AZURE INTERVIEW QUESTIONS AND ANSWERS

460 Real World Scenerios & Answers

KS EBOOKS

Copyright © 2023 by Ks Ks (Ks Ebooks & Materials).

All rights reserved. No part of this book may be used or reproduced in any form whatsoever without written permission except in the case of brief quotations in critical articles or reviews.

For more information, or to book an event, contact :

http://www.ksebooks.com

AZURE INTERVIEW QUESTIONS

CONTENTS

AZURE INTERVIEW QUESTIONS AND ANSWERS I

CONTENTS..2

ABOUT THEEBOOK 216

CHAPTER 1

AZURE

REAL-WORLD SCENARIOS

Scenario:

Q1: Question: How can I deploy a web application on Azure?

Answer: To deploy a web application on Azure, you can use Azure App Service. You can create an App Service plan, which represents the resources allocated to host your web application. Then, you can create an App Service instance within the plan and publish your web application code using FTP, Git, or Azure DevOps. Azure App Service takes care of the infrastructure and platform management, allowing you to focus on your application.

Scenario:

Q2: Question: How can I scale my Azure Virtual Machines (VMs) based on demand?

Answer: Azure Virtual Machine Scale Sets provide an easy way to automatically scale your VMs based on demand. You can define scaling rules based on metrics like CPU utilization or network traffic. When the specified threshold is reached, Azure will automatically add or remove VM instances to match the desired scale. This allows your application to handle increased traffic during peak times and reduce costs during periods of low demand.

Scenario:

Q3: Question: How can I ensure the availability and resilience of my Azure resources?

Answer: Azure offers several services and features to ensure the availability and resilience of your resources. One common approach is to use Azure Availability Zones, which are physically separate data centers within an Azure region. By distributing your resources across multiple availability zones, you can protect against data center failures. Additionally, Azure provides services like Azure Load Balancer, Azure Traffic Manager, and Azure Application Gateway to distribute traffic and ensure high availability of your applications.

Scenario:

Q4: Question: How can I secure my Azure virtual networks?

Answer: To secure your Azure virtual networks, you can implement various measures. One important step is to use Network Security Groups (NSGs) to control inbound and outbound traffic at the network level. NSGs allow you to define access control rules based on source/destination IP addresses, ports, and protocols. You can also use Azure Virtual Network Service Endpoints to securely access Azure services over a private network connection, without exposing them to the public internet.

Scenario:

Q5: Question: How can I analyze and gain insights from my data using Azure?

Answer: Azure offers several services for data analysis and gaining insights. Azure Synapse Analytics provides a unified analytics experience, combining big data and data warehousing capabilities. You can use Azure Machine Learning to build and deploy machine learning models for predictive analytics. Azure Data Factory helps you orchestrate and automate data workflows, and Azure Databricks provides a collaborative environment for big data analytics and AI.

Scenario:

Q6: Question: How can I automate the deployment of Azure resources?

Answer: You can use Azure Resource Manager (ARM) templates to automate the deployment of Azure resources. ARM templates are JSON files that define the desired state of your infrastructure. You can specify the resources, their configurations, and any dependencies. By deploying the template, Azure will provision the resources and ensure they are set up according to the defined specifications. You can deploy ARM templates using Azure Portal, Azure CLI, PowerShell, or Azure DevOps.

Scenario:

Q7: Question: How can I monitor the performance and health of my Azure resources?

Answer: Azure provides various monitoring and diagnostics services. Azure Monitor allows you to collect and analyze telemetry data from your resources, including metrics, logs, and alerts. You can set up alerts based on specific conditions, such as CPU utilization exceeding a threshold. Azure Application Insights provides application performance monitoring, including request tracking, performance counters, and exception tracking. Azure Log Analytics enables centralized log collection and analysis across multiple resources.

Scenario:

Q8: Question: How can I implement disaster recovery for my Azure VMs?

Answer: Azure Site Recovery is a service that enables disaster recovery for Azure VMs and on-premises workloads. By replicating VMs to a secondary Azure region, you can ensure business continuity in the event of an outage. Azure Site Recovery provides continuous replication and automated recovery, allowing you to failover to the secondary region when needed. It supports both Windows and Linux VMs and provides options for testing failover and planned failover scenarios.

Scenario:

Q9: Question: How can I secure and manage identities in Azure?

Answer: Azure Active Directory (Azure AD) is a cloud-based identity and access management service in Azure. It provides features for managing user identities, securing access to resources, and integrating with other applications. You can use Azure AD for single sign-on, multi-factor authentication, role-based access control (RBAC), and identity federation. Azure AD can be used to authenticate and authorize access to Azure resources, as well as external applications and services integrated with Azure.

Scenario:

Q10: Question: How can I store and analyze large amounts of data in Azure?

Answer: Azure offers several services for storing and analyzing large data sets. Azure Storage provides scalable and durable object storage for various types of data. Azure Data Lake Storage is designed for big data analytics, allowing you to store and process massive amounts of structured and unstructured data. For analysis, you can use Azure HDInsight, which is a managed big data service supporting popular analytics frameworks like Hadoop, Spark, and Hive.

Scenario:

Q11: Question: How can I deploy a containerized application on Azure?

Answer: Azure provides Azure Kubernetes Service (AKS), a fully managed container orchestration service. You can deploy your containerized application to AKS by creating a Kubernetes cluster. AKS takes care of managing the underlying infrastructure, and you can use tools like kubectl or Azure CLI to deploy your application containers, define scaling rules, and manage the lifecycle of your application.

Scenario:

Q12: Question: How can I integrate Azure services with my existing on-premises infrastructure?

Answer: Azure offers several options for integrating with on-premises infrastructure. Azure Virtual Network allows you to establish a secure connection between your on-premises network and Azure using Azure VPN Gateway or ExpressRoute. Azure Hybrid Connections enable secure and seamless connectivity between Azure and your on-premises resources without requiring any network changes. You can also use Azure Service Bus to facilitate messaging and communication between on-premises systems and Azure services.

Scenario:

Q13: Question: How can I automate the management and configuration of my Azure resources?

Answer: Azure Automation provides a set of services for automating the management and configuration of Azure resources. You can use Azure Automation Runbooks, which are PowerShell or Python scripts, to define and execute tasks. These tasks can include resource provisioning, configuration management, and monitoring actions. Azure Automation also supports scheduling, so you can automate the execution of scripts at specific times or trigger them based on events.

Scenario:

Q14: Question: How can I secure and protect my data in Azure?

Answer: Azure provides various security features to protect your data. Azure Key Vault allows you to securely store and manage cryptographic keys, secrets, and certificates. You can use Azure Disk Encryption to encrypt the data on your Azure VMs. Azure Information Protection helps you classify and protect sensitive information by applying labels and rights management policies. Azure Security Center provides security recommendations, threat detection, and incident response for your Azure resources.

Scenario:

Q15: Question: How can I enable global distribution and high availability for my web application?

Answer: Azure Content Delivery Network (CDN) can help enable global distribution and improve the performance of your web application. By caching content at edge locations around the world, CDN reduces latency and improves the user experience. Azure Traffic Manager can be used to distribute user traffic across multiple endpoints in different Azure regions, ensuring high availability and disaster recovery. You can also leverage Azure Front Door, which provides global load balancing and application acceleration capabilities.

Scenario:

Q16: Question: How can I implement serverless computing in Azure?

Answer: Azure Functions is a serverless computing service in Azure. With Azure Functions, you can write code in a supported language (such as C#, JavaScript, or Python) and execute it in a serverless environment. Functions can be triggered by various events, such as HTTP requests, timer schedules, or messages from Azure services. Azure Functions automatically scales and manages the underlying infrastructure, allowing you to focus on writing the business logic of your application.

Scenario:

Q17: Question: How can I store and manage structured data in Azure?

Answer: Azure offers Azure SQL Database, a fully managed relational database service. Azure SQL Database provides a scalable and highly available platform for storing and managing structured data. It supports Transact-SQL (T-SQL) and provides features like automatic patching, backups, and built-in high availability. Azure also offers other database services like Azure Database for MySQL, Azure Database for PostgreSQL, and Azure Cosmos DB for NoSQL and globally distributed databases.

Scenario:

Q18: Question: How can I analyze and visualize data in real-time using Azure?

Answer: Azure Stream Analytics is a real-time analytics and event-processing service in Azure. You can use Azure Stream Analytics to ingest, process, and analyze streaming data from various sources, such as IoT devices or application logs. The service supports querying data using a SQL-like language and provides integration with other Azure services like Azure Event Hubs and Azure Cosmos DB. You can also use Power BI, a powerful business intelligence and data visualization tool, to create interactive dashboards and reports based on your analyzed data.

Scenario:

Q19: Question: How can I protect my Azure virtual machines from malware and threats?

Answer: Azure Security Center provides advanced threat protection for Azure virtual machines. It uses machine learning and behavioral analytics to detect and respond to threats. Security Center can provide recommendations for improving the security posture of your VMs and help you remediate vulnerabilities. Additionally, you can use Azure Security Center to enable just-in-time (JIT) access, which limits the exposure of your VMs by only allowing access when needed and for a limited time.

Scenario:

Q20: Question: How can I implement a highly available and scalable database solution in Azure?

Answer: Azure Cosmos DB is a globally distributed, multi-model database service that provides high availability and scalability. It offers multiple consistency models, such as strong, bounded staleness, and eventual consistency, to meet different application requirements. Cosmos DB supports various data models, including key-value, document, graph, and column-family, and it automatically indexes data for fast querying. You can also scale throughput and storage independently to handle high traffic loads.

Scenario:

Q21: Question: How can I implement a data backup and recovery solution in Azure?

Answer: Azure Backup is a service that enables you to back up and restore your data in Azure. You can use Azure Backup to protect various types of data, including files, folders, virtual machines, and Azure SQL databases. It provides automated backups, encryption, and long-term retention options. You can define backup policies, schedule backups, and easily restore data when needed.

Scenario:

Q22: Question: How can I ensure compliance and meet regulatory requirements in Azure?

Answer: Azure offers various services and features to help you achieve compliance and meet regulatory requirements. Azure Policy allows you to define and enforce rules and standards across your Azure resources. Azure Security Center provides compliance assessments and recommendations based on industry standards.

Azure Governance provides features like resource tagging and management groups to organize and govern your resources. Additionally, Azure offers compliance certifications and documentation to support your compliance efforts.

Scenario:

Q23: Question: How can I implement continuous integration and continuous deployment (CI/CD) for my applications in Azure?

Answer: Azure DevOps is a comprehensive set of development tools and services that enable CI/CD pipelines. You can use Azure Pipelines, a part of Azure DevOps, to build, test, and deploy your applications to Azure. With Azure Pipelines, you can define automated workflows, integrate with source control systems like Git, and deploy to various Azure services. Azure Pipelines supports multiple programming languages and platforms, providing flexibility for your CI/CD needs.

Scenario:

Q24: Question: How can I integrate Azure services with third-party applications and services?

Answer: Azure offers a range of integration options for connecting with third-party applications and services. Azure Logic Apps provides a visual design surface for building workflows and integrating systems using pre-built connectors for popular services.

Azure Service Bus enables reliable messaging and event-driven communication between applications and services. Azure Event Grid allows you to react to events and trigger actions in real-time. Additionally, Azure API Management provides a comprehensive solution for managing and publishing APIs.

Scenario:

Q25: Question: How can I optimize costs and right-size my Azure resources?

Answer: Azure provides several tools and features to help you optimize costs. Azure Cost Management + Billing allows you to monitor and analyze your Azure costs, set budgets, and receive cost alerts. Azure Advisor provides recommendations for optimizing your resource utilization, such as right-sizing VMs or leveraging reserved instances. Azure Virtual Machine Scale Sets and Azure Functions can automatically scale resources based on demand, helping you optimize costs during periods of low usage.

Scenario:

Q26: Question: How can I implement a high-performance and scalable storage solution in Azure?

Answer: Azure offers various storage options to meet different performance and scalability needs. Azure Blob Storage is a scalable object storage service for storing large amounts of unstructured data. Azure Files provides fully managed file shares accessible via the SMB protocol. Azure Disk Storage offers persistent, high-performance block storage for Azure VMs. Azure Data Lake Storage provides a scalable and secure solution for big data analytics. You can choose the appropriate storage option based on your specific requirements.

Scenario:

Q27: Question: How can I monitor and optimize the performance of my Azure resources?

Answer: Azure Monitor provides a centralized platform for monitoring the performance of your Azure resources. It collects and analyzes telemetry data, including metrics, logs, and traces. With Azure Monitor, you can set up alerts based on predefined conditions or custom queries, create dashboards for visualization, and perform deep analysis to identify performance bottlenecks. Additionally, Azure Advisor provides recommendations for optimizing the performance and efficiency of your resources.

Scenario:

Q28: Question: How can I implement a secure and scalable Internet of Things (IoT) solution in Azure?

Answer: Azure IoT Hub is a managed service that enables secure communication and management of IoT devices. You can connect, provision, and monitor IoT devices at scale using IoT Hub. It provides device-to-cloud and cloud-to-device messaging, device management capabilities, and integration with other Azure services for data processing and analytics. Azure IoT Central is a fully managed SaaS solution that simplifies the deployment and management of IoT applications.

Scenario:

Q29: Question: How can I implement a serverless data warehouse solution in Azure?

Answer: Azure Synapse Analytics, formerly known as Azure SQL Data Warehouse, is a serverless and massively parallel processing (MPP) data warehousing service. It allows you to analyze large volumes of structured and unstructured data using standard SQL queries. With Synapse Analytics, you can ingest, prepare, manage, and serve data for business intelligence and analytics purposes. It provides integration with various Azure services and supports on-demand and provisioned resource scaling to handle workload requirements.

Scenario:

Q30: Question: How can I ensure data sovereignty and compliance with data residency requirements in Azure?

Answer: Azure provides options to ensure data sovereignty and compliance with data residency requirements. Azure offers a wide range of datacenter regions across the globe, allowing you to choose the specific region where your data is stored. Additionally, Azure offers Azure Sovereign Clouds, such as Azure Government, designed to meet the specific compliance and data residency needs of government and highly regulated industries.

Scenario:

Q31: Question: How can I implement real-time analytics and machine learning on streaming data in Azure?

Answer: Azure Stream Analytics provides a real-time analytics and event-processing service in Azure. You can use Stream Analytics to process and analyze streaming data from various sources, such as IoT devices or social media streams. It supports SQL-like queries and allows you to apply real-time analytics and machine learning models to the data. You can leverage Azure Machine Learning to build and deploy machine learning models, and integrate them with Stream Analytics for real-time scoring and insights.

Scenario:

Q32: Question: How can I implement a serverless API backend in Azure?

Answer: Azure Functions and Azure API Management can be used together to implement a serverless API backend in Azure. Azure Functions allows you to create serverless compute resources that can be used to handle API requests and execute the necessary business logic. Azure API Management provides a comprehensive platform to manage and secure your APIs, including features like authentication, rate limiting, and caching. You can expose your Azure Functions as APIs through Azure API Management, providing a scalable and managed API solution.

Scenario:

Q33: Question: How can I implement a disaster recovery solution for my Azure SQL databases?

Answer: Azure SQL Database provides built-in capabilities for disaster recovery. You can configure geo-replication for your Azure SQL databases to replicate data to a secondary region. In the event of a disaster, you can failover to the secondary region and continue operations. Azure SQL Database also supports automatic backups, point-in-time restore, and long-term retention options, allowing you to recover from accidental data loss or corruption.

Scenario:

Q34: Question: How can I implement a serverless data processing pipeline in Azure?

Answer: Azure Data Factory is a fully managed service that allows you to create serverless data processing pipelines. You can use Data Factory to orchestrate and automate the movement and transformation of data from various sources to target destinations. It supports data integration, data movement, and data transformation activities. You can schedule pipelines, monitor and manage data flows, and integrate with other Azure services for advanced data processing scenarios.

Scenario:

Q35: Question: How can I implement a secure and scalable identity and access management solution in Azure?

Answer: Azure Active Directory (Azure AD) provides a comprehensive identity and access management solution in Azure. Azure AD supports user management, single sign-on (SSO), multi-factor authentication (MFA), and role-based access control (RBAC). You can use Azure AD to authenticate and authorize access to your applications and resources in Azure. It also integrates with other identity providers, such as on-premises Active Directory or social identity providers, to enable federated authentication.

Scenario:

Q36: Question: How can I implement a scalable and fault-tolerant messaging system in Azure?

Answer: Azure Service Bus is a fully managed messaging service that enables reliable and asynchronous communication between applications and services. You can use Service Bus to decouple components of your system, ensure message reliability, and enable scalable message processing. Service Bus supports various messaging patterns, such as publish/subscribe and request/response, and provides features like message ordering, dead-lettering, and duplicate detection.

Scenario:

Q37: Question: How can I implement a serverless data integration and orchestration solution in Azure?

Answer: Azure Logic Apps is a serverless integration and workflow orchestration service in Azure. You can use Logic Apps to build workflows that integrate and automate processes across different systems and services. Logic Apps provides a wide range of connectors for popular applications and services, allowing you to easily create workflows that handle data integration, transformation, and orchestration tasks. You can also leverage the built-in control flow logic and triggers to create powerful serverless workflows.

Scenario:

Q38: Question: How can I implement a geographically distributed database in Azure?

Answer: Azure Cosmos DB is a globally distributed, multi-model database service that provides automatic scaling, low latency, and guaranteed high availability. You can choose the consistency model and data model (e.g., document, key-value, graph) that best suits your application. Cosmos DB automatically replicates and synchronizes data across multiple Azure regions, allowing you to achieve low-latency access and high availability across different geographical locations.

Scenario:

Q39: Question: How can I implement a secure and scalable container registry in Azure?

Answer: Azure Container Registry is a managed, private Docker container registry that allows you to store and manage your container images. You can use Azure Container Registry to store and organize your container images securely. It provides authentication and access control mechanisms to control who can pull and push container images. Azure Container Registry integrates seamlessly with Azure Kubernetes Service (AKS) and other container orchestrators, enabling you to easily deploy and manage your containerized applications.

Scenario:

Q40: Question: How can I implement serverless event-driven architectures in Azure?

AZURE INTERVIEW QUESTIONS

Answer: Azure Event Grid is a fully managed event routing service that simplifies the development of event-driven architectures. You can use Event Grid to react to events and trigger actions in real-time. It provides a publish-subscribe model where event publishers send events to Event Grid, and event subscribers handle the events based on their subscriptions. Event Grid supports a wide range of event sources and destinations, including Azure services, custom HTTP endpoints, and third-party applications.

Scenario:

Q41: Question: How can I implement a scalable and distributed cache in Azure?

Answer: Azure Cache for Redis is a fully managed, distributed cache service in Azure. You can use Azure Cache for Redis to improve the performance and scalability of your applications by caching frequently accessed data. It supports in-memory caching and provides advanced features like data persistence, clustering, and high availability. You can integrate Azure Cache for Redis with your applications using various Redis clients and SDKs.

Scenario:

Q42: Question: How can I implement a serverless event-driven architecture for IoT devices in Azure?

Answer: Azure Event Grid and Azure IoT Hub can be used together to implement a serverless event-driven architecture for IoT devices in Azure. Azure IoT Hub provides device-to-cloud and cloud-to-device messaging, device management, and secure connectivity for IoT devices. You can connect your IoT devices to IoT Hub, and then use Azure Event Grid to react to events generated by the devices. This allows you to process and act upon IoT device events in real-time.

Scenario:

Q43: Question: How can I implement a secure and scalable file storage solution in Azure?

Answer: Azure Files is a fully managed, cloud-based file storage service in Azure. You can use Azure Files to create file shares that can be accessed from multiple virtual machines and applications. Azure Files supports standard SMB file sharing protocols and provides features like encryption at rest, Azure Active Directory integration for authentication, and access control through shared access signatures (SAS). It offers scalable storage capacity and performance to meet your file storage needs.

Scenario:

Q44: Question: How can I implement a serverless data transformation and ETL (Extract, Transform, Load) process in

AZURE INTERVIEW QUESTIONS

Azure?

Answer: Azure Data Factory is a fully managed service that allows you to create serverless data transformation and ETL pipelines. You can use Data Factory to orchestrate and automate the movement, transformation, and processing of data from various sources to target destinations. It supports data integration, data movement, and data transformation activities, and provides connectors to a wide range of data sources and sinks. You can schedule and monitor the execution of data pipelines in Data Factory.

Scenario:

Q45: Question: How can I implement a secure and scalable API gateway in Azure?

Answer: Azure API Management is a fully managed service that enables you to create, publish, secure, and monitor APIs. You can use Azure API Management as a gateway for your APIs, providing centralized access control, rate limiting, caching, and analytics. It allows you to enforce policies, such as authentication and authorization, and provides developer portal capabilities for documentation and self-service registration. Azure API Management integrates with Azure Functions, Azure Logic Apps, and other backend services to create a comprehensive API management solution.

Scenario:

Q46: Question: How can I implement a serverless data ingestion and processing pipeline in Azure?

Answer: Azure Event Hubs and Azure Functions can be used together to implement a serverless data ingestion and processing pipeline in Azure. Azure Event Hubs is a highly scalable and distributed event streaming platform that can handle millions of events per second. You can use Event Hubs to ingest data from various sources in real-time. Azure Functions provides serverless compute resources that can be triggered by events in Event Hubs. You can write event-driven functions that process and analyze the ingested data.

Scenario:

Q47: Question: How can I implement a serverless search solution in Azure?

Answer: Azure Cognitive Search is a fully managed search-as-a-service solution in Azure. You can use Azure Cognitive Search to build search experiences over structured and unstructured data. It supports full-text search, faceted navigation, and advanced search capabilities. You can index data from various sources, including Azure Blob Storage, Azure SQL Database, and Azure Cosmos DB. Azure Cognitive Search provides features like indexing pipelines, search indexes, and search APIs to enable powerful search functionality in your applications.

Scenario:

Q48: Question: How can I implement a scalable and reliable messaging system for microservices in Azure?

Answer: Azure Service Bus and Azure Kubernetes Service (AKS) can be used together to implement a scalable and reliable messaging system for microservices in Azure. Azure Service Bus provides messaging capabilities that allow microservices to communicate asynchronously. You can use Service Bus queues or topics to decouple the components of your system. Azure Kubernetes Service (AKS) provides a managed Kubernetes environment for deploying and scaling containerized applications. You can deploy your microservices as containers in AKS and use Service Bus to enable communication between them.

Scenario:

Q49: Question: How can I implement a serverless data analytics solution in Azure?

Answer: Azure Synapse Analytics (formerly Azure SQL Data Warehouse) and Azure Databricks can be used together to implement a serverless data analytics solution in Azure. Azure Synapse Analytics is a fully managed and scalable analytics service that allows you to analyze large volumes of data using standard

SQL queries. Azure Databricks is an Apache Spark-based analytics platform that provides advanced analytics and machine learning capabilities. You can leverage Synapse Analytics for data warehousing and SQL-based analytics, and integrate it with Databricks for advanced data processing and machine learning.

Scenario:

Q50: Question: How can I implement a secure and scalable identity federation solution in Azure?

Answer: Azure Active Directory (Azure AD) and Azure AD B2C can be used together to implement a secure and scalable identity federation solution in Azure. Azure AD provides a comprehensive identity and access management solution for organizations, supporting single sign-on (SSO) and access control across applications and services. Azure AD B2C is a cloud-based identity service that enables customer-facing applications to authenticate and authorize users. You can use Azure AD for employee and organizational identity management, and Azure AD B2C for external customer identity management.

Scenario:

Q51: Question: How can I implement a serverless data visualization and reporting solution in Azure?

Answer: Azure Power BI is a cloud-based business intelligence service that allows you to create interactive data visualizations and reports. You can use Power BI to connect to various data sources, transform and model the data, and create visualizations and dashboards. Power BI integrates with Azure services and other data sources, providing real-time insights and data-driven decision-making capabilities. You can embed Power BI reports and dashboards into your applications or share them securely with others.

Scenario:

Q52: Question: How can I implement a serverless media processing and streaming solution in Azure?

Answer: Azure Media Services is a cloud-based platform that enables the encoding, streaming, and delivery of media content. You can use Media Services to process and transform media files into various formats suitable for streaming or on-demand playback. It provides capabilities for live and on-demand video streaming, content protection with digital rights management (DRM), and dynamic packaging for adaptive streaming. You can integrate Media Services with other Azure services and use APIs or SDKs to manage and deliver media content.

Scenario:

Q53: Question: How can I implement a scalable and secure Internet of Things (IoT) analytics solution in Azure?

Answer: Azure IoT Central and Azure Time Series Insights can be used together to implement a scalable and secure IoT analytics solution in Azure. Azure IoT Central is a fully managed SaaS solution that simplifies the deployment and management of IoT applications. It provides built-in capabilities for device management, telemetry ingestion, and visualization of IoT data. Azure Time Series Insights is a scalable and fully managed service that allows you to store, analyze, and visualize time series data from IoT devices. You can integrate IoT Central with Time Series Insights to gain valuable insights and perform advanced analytics on your IoT data.

Scenario:

Q54: Question: How can I implement a serverless document processing solution in Azure?

Answer: Azure Form Recognizer and Azure Logic Apps can be used together to implement a serverless document processing solution in Azure. Azure Form Recognizer is a cognitive service that uses machine learning to extract data from forms and documents. You can train the Form Recognizer model to recognize and extract specific fields from your documents. Azure Logic Apps provides a visual workflow designer that allows you to create automated document processing workflows. You can use Logic Apps to trigger document processing based on events, extract data using Form Recognizer, and integrate with other services for further processing or storage.

Scenario:

Q55: Question: How can I implement a secure and scalable data lake solution in Azure?

Answer: Azure Data Lake Storage is a scalable and secure data lake storage service in Azure. You can use Data Lake Storage to store and analyze large volumes of structured and unstructured data. It provides high throughput, parallel access, and strong security features. You can leverage Azure Data Lake Analytics to process and analyze data stored in Data Lake Storage using U-SQL or Spark. Azure Data Lake Storage integrates with various Azure services and tools, enabling you to build end-to-end data lake solutions.

Scenario:

Q56: Question: How can I implement a serverless data warehousing solution in Azure?

Answer: Azure Synapse Analytics is a fully managed analytics service that combines data warehousing, big data, and data integration into a single unified platform. You can use Azure Synapse Analytics to store and analyze large volumes of structured and unstructured data. It provides features like distributed query processing, data lake integration, and built-in machine learning capabilities. You can leverage Synapse Analytics to ingest, transform, and analyze data from various sources, and gain insights for decision-making.

Scenario:

Q57: Question: How can I implement a serverless natural language processing (NLP) solution in Azure?

Answer: Azure Cognitive Services, specifically Language Understanding (LUIS) and Text Analytics, can be used together to implement a serverless natural language processing solution in Azure. LUIS allows you to build language understanding models that extract intent and entities from text. Text Analytics provides capabilities for sentiment analysis, key phrase extraction, and entity recognition. You can integrate LUIS and Text Analytics into your applications or workflows to enable language understanding and analysis of text-based data.

Scenario:

Q58: Question: How can I implement a serverless batch processing solution in Azure?

Answer: Azure Batch and Azure Functions can be used together to implement a serverless batch processing solution in Azure. Azure Batch is a fully managed service that allows you to run large-scale parallel and high-performance computing (HPC) batch jobs. You can define and submit batch jobs to Azure Batch, and it will handle the provisioning and management of compute resources. Azure Functions provides serverless compute resources that can be triggered by events. You can write event-driven functions that process individual tasks within the batch job.

Scenario:

Q59: Question: How can I implement a secure and scalable data encryption solution in Azure?

Answer: Azure Key Vault is a cloud-based service that allows you to securely store and manage cryptographic keys, secrets, and certificates. You can use Azure Key Vault to protect sensitive data and encrypt your applications and services. Key Vault provides integration with Azure services and allows you to securely retrieve and use cryptographic keys and secrets. It also offers features like key rotation, auditing, and access control, ensuring the security and compliance of your data.

Scenario:

Q60: Question: How can I implement a serverless internet-scale event processing solution in Azure?

Answer: Azure Event Grid and Azure Functions can be used together to implement a serverless internet-scale event processing solution in Azure. Azure Event Grid provides an event-routing service that allows you to react to events and trigger actions in real-time. Azure Functions provides serverless compute resources that can be triggered by events. You can use Event Grid to receive events from various sources and route them to Azure Functions for event processing and action execution.

Scenario:

Q61: Question: How can I implement a serverless machine learning solution in Azure?

Answer: Azure Machine Learning is a cloud-based service that allows you to build, deploy, and manage machine learning models at scale. You can use Azure Machine Learning to train and deploy models using a variety of frameworks and tools. It provides capabilities for data preparation, model training, and model deployment in a serverless environment. You can leverage Azure Machine Learning to build intelligent applications and make predictions based on your data.

Scenario:

Q62: Question: How can I implement a serverless geospatial analysis solution in Azure?

Answer: Azure Maps and Azure Functions can be used together to implement a serverless geospatial analysis solution in Azure. Azure

AZURE INTERVIEW QUESTIONS

Maps is a set of geospatial APIs that enable you to build mapping and location-based services. Azure Functions provides serverless compute resources that can be triggered by events. You can use Azure Maps APIs to perform geospatial analysis and visualization, and trigger Azure Functions based on location-based events.

Scenario:

Q63: Question: How can I implement a scalable and secure IoT device provisioning solution in Azure?

Answer: Azure IoT Hub and Azure Device Provisioning Service (DPS) can be used together to implement a scalable and secure IoT device provisioning solution in Azure. Azure IoT Hub provides device-to-cloud and cloud-to-device messaging, device management, and secure connectivity for IoT devices. Azure DPS is a fully managed service that simplifies the provisioning of IoT devices at scale. You can use DPS to securely provision and register devices with IoT Hub, ensuring their identity and access control.

Scenario:

Q64: Question: How can I implement a serverless data archiving and retention solution in Azure?

Answer: Azure Blob Storage and Azure Event Grid can be used together to implement a serverless data archiving and retention solution in Azure. Azure Blob Storage is a scalable and durable object storage service that allows you to store and retrieve large amounts of unstructured data. Azure Event Grid provides an event-routing service that allows you to react to events and trigger actions. You can use Event Grid to listen for data change events in Blob Storage and trigger archiving or retention actions based on specified rules.

Scenario:

Q65: Question: How can I implement a secure and scalable identity and access management solution in Azure?

Answer: Azure Active Directory (Azure AD) and Azure AD B2C can be used together to implement a secure and scalable identity and access management solution in Azure. Azure AD provides a comprehensive identity and access management solution for organizations, supporting single sign-on (SSO) and access control across applications and services. Azure AD B2C is a cloud-based identity service that enables customer-facing applications to authenticate and authorize users. You can use Azure AD for employee and organizational identity management, and Azure AD B2C for external customer identity management.

Scenario:

Q66: Question: How can I implement a serverless data integration and orchestration solution in Azure?

AZURE INTERVIEW QUESTIONS

Answer: Azure Data Factory is a cloud-based data integration service that allows you to create data-driven workflows for orchestrating and automating data movement and transformation. You can use Azure Data Factory to build data pipelines that can integrate data from various sources, transform it as needed, and load it into target data stores. It provides a visual interface for designing and monitoring data pipelines and supports a wide range of data sources and destinations.

Scenario:

Q67: Question: How can I implement a serverless image recognition and analysis solution in Azure?

Answer: Azure Cognitive Services, specifically Computer Vision and Custom Vision, can be used together to implement a serverless image recognition and analysis solution in Azure. Computer Vision provides pre-built models for image recognition, object detection, and image analysis. Custom Vision allows you to train custom models using your own image datasets. You can integrate these services into your applications or workflows to perform image recognition, object detection, and other image analysis tasks.

Scenario:

Q68: Question: How can I implement a serverless log processing and analysis solution in Azure?

Answer: Azure Log Analytics and Azure Functions can be used together to implement a serverless log processing and analysis solution in Azure. Azure Log Analytics is a service that collects and analyzes log data from various sources, including virtual machines, containers, and applications. Azure Functions provides serverless compute resources that can be triggered by events. You can use Log Analytics to collect log data and trigger Azure Functions for log processing, analysis, and alerting based on specified rules.

Scenario:

Q69: Question: How can I implement a serverless content delivery solution in Azure?

Answer: Azure Content Delivery Network (CDN) is a globally distributed network of servers that helps deliver content to users with low latency and high performance. You can use Azure CDN to cache and deliver static content, such as images, videos, and web pages, from locations close to your users. It provides features like dynamic site acceleration, content compression, and HTTPS support. You can integrate Azure CDN with your applications or websites to improve content delivery speed and user experience.

Scenario:

Q70: Question: How can I implement a serverless predictive maintenance solution in Azure?

Answer: Azure IoT Hub and Azure Machine Learning can be used together to implement a serverless predictive maintenance solution in Azure. Azure IoT Hub provides device-to-cloud and cloud-to-device messaging, device management, and secure connectivity for IoT devices. Azure Machine Learning allows you to build, deploy, and manage machine learning models. You can use IoT Hub to ingest telemetry data from IoT devices, send it to Azure Machine Learning for analysis, and leverage machine learning models to predict maintenance needs and optimize maintenance schedules.

Scenario:

Q71: Question: How can I implement a serverless data streaming and real-time analytics solution in Azure?

Answer: Azure Stream Analytics is a real-time analytics service that allows you to process and analyze streaming data from various sources, such as IoT devices, social media, and application logs. You can use Azure Stream Analytics to perform real-time data transformations, aggregations, and complex event processing. It integrates with Azure services like Event Hubs and IoT Hub to ingest and process streaming data. You can leverage Stream Analytics to gain insights from your streaming data in real-time.

Scenario:

Q72: Question: How can I implement a serverless video transcoding and streaming solution in Azure?

Answer: Azure Media Services and Azure Functions can be used together to implement a serverless video transcoding and streaming solution in Azure. Azure Media Services is a cloud-based platform that enables encoding, streaming, and delivery of media content. You can use Azure Media Services to transcode video files into various formats suitable for streaming or on-demand playback. Azure Functions provides serverless compute resources that can be triggered by events. You can use Functions to automate the transcoding process and trigger streaming events based on specific conditions.

Scenario:

Q73: Question: How can I implement a scalable and secure data backup and recovery solution in Azure?

Answer: Azure Backup is a cloud-based backup service that allows you to protect and recover your data from various sources, such as virtual machines, databases, and file servers. You can use Azure Backup to schedule regular backups, retain backups for long-term retention, and restore data when needed. It provides features like encryption, compression, and incremental backups to optimize storage usage. You can integrate Azure Backup with other Azure services to create a comprehensive data protection and recovery strategy.

AZURE INTERVIEW QUESTIONS

Scenario:

Q74: Question: How can I implement a serverless anomaly detection and alerting solution in Azure?

Answer: Azure Machine Learning and Azure Monitor can be used together to implement a serverless anomaly detection and alerting solution in Azure. Azure Machine Learning allows you to build, deploy, and manage machine learning models. Azure Monitor is a monitoring and alerting service that collects and analyzes telemetry data from various Azure resources. You can use Azure Machine Learning to train models for anomaly detection, and Azure Monitor to ingest and analyze telemetry data and trigger alerts based on detected anomalies.

Scenario:

Q75: Question: How can I implement a serverless customer engagement and personalization solution in Azure?

Answer: Azure Personalizer and Azure Logic Apps can be used together to implement a serverless customer engagement and personalization solution in Azure. Azure Personalizer is a cloud-based service that allows you to create personalized user experiences by ranking and selecting the most relevant content or actions. Azure Logic Apps provides a visual workflow designer that allows you to create automated workflows for integrating and orchestrating services. You can use Logic Apps to trigger personalized engagements based on user interactions and data, and leverage Personalizer to optimize and personalize the content or actions delivered to users.

Scenario:

Q76: Question: How can I implement a serverless data visualization solution in Azure?

Answer: Azure Synapse Analytics and Power BI can be used together to implement a serverless data visualization solution in Azure. Azure Synapse Analytics is a unified analytics service that integrates big data and data warehousing capabilities. It allows you to ingest, prepare, manage, and serve data for immediate business intelligence and data visualization needs. Power BI is a business analytics service that provides interactive visualizations and reports. You can connect Power BI to Azure Synapse Analytics to create visually appealing and interactive dashboards and reports based on your data.

Scenario:

Q77: Question: How can I implement a serverless document processing solution in Azure?

Answer: Azure Form Recognizer and Azure Logic Apps can be used together to implement a serverless document processing solution in Azure. Azure Form Recognizer is a service that uses machine learning to extract structured data from documents. It can analyze various document types, such as invoices, receipts, and forms, and extract information like fields, tables, and key-value pairs. Azure Logic Apps provides a visual workflow designer that allows you to create automated workflows for integrating and processing data. You can use Logic Apps to trigger document processing based on specific events and leverage Form Recognizer to extract structured data from the documents.

Scenario:

Q78: Question: How can I implement a serverless data lake solution in Azure?

Answer: Azure Data Lake Storage and Azure Databricks can be used together to implement a serverless data lake solution in Azure. Azure Data Lake Storage is a scalable and secure data lake service that allows you to store and analyze large amounts of structured and unstructured data. Azure Databricks is an Apache Spark-based analytics platform that provides a collaborative environment for big data analytics and machine learning. You can use Databricks to process and analyze data stored in Azure Data Lake Storage and leverage its distributed computing capabilities for scalable data processing.

Scenario:

Q79: Question: How can I implement a serverless sentiment

analysis solution in Azure?

Answer: Azure Cognitive Services, specifically Text Analytics and Azure Logic Apps, can be used together to implement a serverless sentiment analysis solution in Azure. Text Analytics provides capabilities for sentiment analysis, key phrase extraction, and entity recognition. Azure Logic Apps provides a visual workflow designer that allows you to create automated workflows for integrating and orchestrating services. You can use Logic Apps to trigger sentiment analysis based on specific events or data inputs, and leverage Text Analytics to analyze the sentiment of text-based data.

Scenario:

Q80: Question: How can I implement a serverless data synchronization solution in Azure?

Answer: Azure Data Sync and Azure Functions can be used together to implement a serverless data synchronization solution in Azure. Azure Data Sync is a service that allows you to synchronize data across multiple Azure databases and on-premises databases. It provides bi-directional data synchronization and conflict resolution capabilities. Azure Functions provides serverless compute resources that can be triggered by events. You can use Functions to automate data synchronization processes and trigger synchronization events based on specific conditions.

AZURE INTERVIEW QUESTIONS

Scenario:

Q81: Question: How can I implement a serverless data streaming and processing solution in Azure?

Answer: Azure Event Hubs and Azure Durable Functions can be used together to implement a serverless data streaming and processing solution in Azure. Azure Event Hubs is a highly scalable and event ingestion service that can handle millions of events per second. It allows you to ingest and store streaming data from various sources. Azure Durable Functions provides serverless compute resources that allow you to build workflows and processes that can react to events. You can use Event Hubs to ingest streaming data and trigger Azure Durable Functions for real-time processing and analysis.

Scenario:

Q82: Question: How can I implement a serverless recommendation system in Azure?

Answer: Azure Machine Learning and Azure Cosmos DB can be used together to implement a serverless recommendation system in Azure. Azure Machine Learning allows you to build, deploy, and manage machine learning models. Azure Cosmos DB is a globally distributed and multi-model database service that can store and query large amounts of data. You can use Azure Machine Learning to train recommendation models based on historical data, and Azure Cosmos DB to store and serve the recommendation data to your applications or users.

Scenario:

Q83: Question: How can I implement a serverless data transformation and enrichment solution in Azure?

Answer: Azure Data Factory and Azure Functions can be used together to implement a serverless data transformation and enrichment solution in Azure. Azure Data Factory is a cloud-based data integration service that allows you to create data-driven workflows for orchestrating and automating data movement and transformation. Azure Functions provides serverless compute resources that can be triggered by events. You can use Azure Data Factory to orchestrate data transformation and enrichment processes, and leverage Azure Functions for custom data processing and enrichment tasks within the workflow.

Scenario:

Q84: Question: How can I implement a serverless natural language processing solution in Azure?

Answer: Azure Cognitive Services, specifically Text Analytics and Language Understanding (LUIS), can be used together to implement a serverless natural language processing solution in

AZURE INTERVIEW QUESTIONS

Azure. Text Analytics provides capabilities for sentiment analysis, key phrase extraction, and entity recognition. LUIS is a machine learning-based service for building natural language understanding into applications. You can use Text Analytics to analyze and extract insights from text-based data, and LUIS to create language understanding models and enable natural language interactions with your applications.

Scenario:

Q85: Question: How can I implement a serverless data warehousing solution in Azure?

Answer: Azure Synapse Analytics, formerly known as Azure SQL Data Warehouse, can be used to implement a serverless data warehousing solution in Azure. Azure Synapse Analytics is an analytics service that combines enterprise data warehousing, big data integration, and data integration. It allows you to store and analyze large volumes of structured and unstructured data. You can use Synapse Analytics to build a data warehouse that can handle complex queries and perform advanced analytics on your data.

Scenario:

Q86: Question: How can I implement a serverless data archiving solution in Azure?

Answer: Azure Blob Storage and Azure Logic Apps can be used together to implement a serverless data archiving solution in Azure. Azure Blob Storage is a scalable and cost-effective storage service that allows you to store large amounts of unstructured data, such as files and backups. Azure Logic Apps provides a visual workflow designer that allows you to create automated workflows for integrating and orchestrating services. You can use Logic Apps to automate the process of archiving data to Azure Blob Storage based on specific events or triggers.

Scenario:

Q87: Question: How can I implement a serverless chatbot solution in Azure?

Answer: Azure Bot Service and Azure Language Understanding (LUIS) can be used together to implement a serverless chatbot solution in Azure. Azure Bot Service is a platform for building and deploying chatbots that can interact with users through multiple channels, such as web, mobile apps, and messaging platforms. Azure Language Understanding (LUIS) is a machine learning-based service for building natural language understanding into applications. You can use LUIS to train models that understand user intents and entities, and integrate it with your chatbot built using Azure Bot Service for intelligent conversation and responses.

Scenario:

AZURE INTERVIEW QUESTIONS

Q88: Question: How can I implement a serverless geospatial analysis solution in Azure?

Answer: Azure Maps and Azure Functions can be used together to implement a serverless geospatial analysis solution in Azure. Azure Maps is a set of location-based services that provide mapping, geocoding, routing, and geospatial analysis capabilities. Azure Functions provides serverless compute resources that can be triggered by events. You can use Azure Functions to build custom geospatial analysis logic and integrate it with Azure Maps for performing geospatial queries, routing optimization, and other geospatial analysis tasks.

Scenario:

Q89: Question: How can I implement a serverless fraud detection solution in Azure?

Answer: Azure Machine Learning and Azure Stream Analytics can be used together to implement a serverless fraud detection solution in Azure. Azure Machine Learning allows you to build, deploy, and manage machine learning models. Azure Stream Analytics is a real-time analytics service that allows you to process and analyze streaming data from various sources. You can use Azure Stream Analytics to ingest and process real-time data, and leverage Azure Machine Learning to detect patterns and anomalies indicative of fraudulent activities in the data.

Scenario:

Q90: Question: How can I implement a serverless data anonymization solution in Azure?

Answer: Azure Data Factory and Azure SQL Database can be used together to implement a serverless data anonymization solution in Azure. Azure Data Factory is a cloud-based data integration service that allows you to create data-driven workflows for orchestrating and automating data movement and transformation. Azure SQL Database is a fully managed relational database service. You can use Azure Data Factory to orchestrate the process of extracting data from the source, applying data anonymization techniques, and loading the anonymized data into Azure SQL Database.

Scenario:

Q91: Question: How can I implement a serverless image recognition solution in Azure?

Answer: Azure Cognitive Services, specifically Computer Vision and Azure Functions, can be used together to implement a serverless image recognition solution in Azure. Computer Vision is a service that provides advanced image analysis capabilities, such as object detection, image classification, and image tagging. Azure Functions provides serverless compute resources that can be triggered by events. You can use Azure Functions to build custom logic that integrates with Computer Vision and processes images in real-time for recognition and analysis.

Scenario:

Q92: Question: How can I implement a serverless data pipeline solution in Azure?

Answer: Azure Data Factory and Azure Databricks can be used together to implement a serverless data pipeline solution in Azure. Azure Data Factory is a cloud-based data integration service that allows you to create data-driven workflows for orchestrating and automating data movement and transformation. Azure Databricks is an Apache Spark-based analytics platform that provides a collaborative environment for big data analytics and machine learning. You can use Data Factory to orchestrate the movement and transformation of data, and leverage Databricks for advanced analytics and processing tasks within the data pipeline.

Scenario:

Q93: Question: How can I implement a serverless document storage and retrieval solution in Azure?

Answer: Azure Blob Storage and Azure Search can be used together to implement a serverless document storage and retrieval solution in Azure. Azure Blob Storage is a scalable and cost-effective storage service that allows you to store and retrieve unstructured data, such as documents, images, and videos. Azure Search is a cloud search service that provides full-text search capabilities over your data. You can store your documents in Azure Blob Storage and use Azure Search to index and search for specific documents based on keywords or other criteria.

Scenario:

Q94: Question: How can I implement a serverless log monitoring and analysis solution in Azure?

Answer: Azure Log Analytics and Azure Monitor can be used together to implement a serverless log monitoring and analysis solution in Azure. Azure Log Analytics is a service that collects, analyzes, and provides insights into log and telemetry data from various sources. Azure Monitor is a monitoring and alerting service that collects and analyzes telemetry data from Azure resources. You can use Azure Log Analytics to centralize and analyze log data, and leverage Azure Monitor to set up alerts and notifications based on specific log events or conditions.

Scenario:

Q95: Question: How can I implement a serverless recommendation engine solution in Azure?

Answer: Azure Machine Learning and Azure Cosmos DB can be used together to implement a serverless recommendation engine solution in Azure. Azure Machine Learning allows you to build, deploy, and manage machine learning models. Azure Cosmos DB is a globally distributed and multi-model database service that can store and query large amounts of data. You can use Azure Machine Learning to train recommendation models based on user behavior and preferences, and Azure Cosmos DB to store and serve the recommendation data for personalized user experiences.

Scenario:

Q96: Question: How can I implement a serverless data backup and restore solution in Azure?

Answer: Azure Backup and Azure Blob Storage can be used together to implement a serverless data backup and restore solution in Azure. Azure Backup is a scalable and secure service that allows you to back up data from various sources, such as virtual machines, databases, and files. Azure Blob Storage is a cost-effective storage service that provides reliable and scalable storage for data backups. You can use Azure Backup to schedule and automate backups, and store the backup data in Azure Blob Storage for easy retrieval and restore when needed.

Scenario:

Q97: Question: How can I implement a serverless IoT data processing solution in Azure?

Answer: Azure IoT Hub and Azure Stream Analytics can be used together to implement a serverless IoT data processing solution in Azure. Azure IoT Hub is a managed service that enables secure and scalable communication between devices and the cloud. Azure Stream Analytics is a real-time analytics service that allows you to process and analyze streaming data from IoT devices. You can use Azure IoT Hub to ingest and manage IoT device data, and leverage Azure Stream Analytics to process and analyze the data in real-time for insights and actions.

Scenario:

Q98: Question: How can I implement a serverless video transcoding solution in Azure?

Answer: Azure Media Services and Azure Functions can be used together to implement a serverless video transcoding solution in Azure. Azure Media Services is a scalable and secure platform that allows you to encode, encrypt, and stream video and audio content at scale. Azure Functions provides serverless compute resources that can be triggered by events. You can use Azure Functions to automate the process of triggering video transcoding jobs in Azure Media Services based on specific events, such as the upload of a new video file, and process the transcoded output as needed.

Scenario:

Q99: Question: How can I implement a serverless data

AZURE INTERVIEW QUESTIONS

anonymization solution in Azure?

Answer: Azure Data Factory and Azure Databricks can be used together to implement a serverless data anonymization solution in Azure. Azure Data Factory is a cloud-based data integration service that allows you to create data-driven workflows for orchestrating and automating data movement and transformation. Azure Databricks is an Apache Spark-based analytics platform that provides a collaborative environment for big data analytics and machine learning. You can use Azure Data Factory to orchestrate the process of extracting data from the source, applying data anonymization techniques using Azure Databricks, and loading the anonymized data into the target destination.

Scenario:

Q100: Question: How can I implement a serverless sentiment analysis solution for social media data in Azure?

Answer: Azure Cognitive Services, specifically Text Analytics and Azure Logic Apps, can be used together to implement a serverless sentiment analysis solution for social media data in Azure. Text Analytics provides capabilities for sentiment analysis, key phrase extraction, and entity recognition. Azure Logic Apps provides a visual workflow designer that allows you to create automated workflows for integrating and orchestrating services. You can use Logic Apps to monitor social media platforms for new posts or mentions, extract the relevant text data, and trigger sentiment analysis using Text Analytics to understand the sentiment expressed in the social media posts.

Scenario:

Q101: Question: How can I implement a serverless data synchronization solution in Azure?

Answer: Azure Data Sync and Azure SQL Database can be used together to implement a serverless data synchronization solution in Azure. Azure Data Sync is a service that enables bi-directional data synchronization between multiple Azure SQL databases and on-premises SQL Server databases. Azure SQL Database is a fully managed relational database service. You can use Azure Data Sync to configure synchronization groups, define sync rules, and automatically synchronize data across multiple databases.

Scenario:

Q102: Question: How can I implement a serverless sentiment analysis solution for customer feedback in Azure?

Answer: Azure Cognitive Services, specifically Text Analytics and Azure Functions, can be used together to implement a serverless sentiment analysis solution for customer feedback in Azure. Text Analytics provides capabilities for sentiment analysis, key phrase extraction, and entity recognition. Azure Functions provides serverless compute resources that can be triggered by events. You can use Azure Functions to build custom logic that integrates with Text Analytics and processes customer feedback in real-time, extracting sentiment scores and generating insights based on the analysis.

Scenario:

Q103: Question: How can I implement a serverless data aggregation and reporting solution in Azure?

Answer: Azure Synapse Analytics and Power BI can be used together to implement a serverless data aggregation and reporting solution in Azure. Azure Synapse Analytics is an analytics service that combines enterprise data warehousing, big data integration, and data integration. Power BI is a business intelligence and data visualization tool. You can use Azure Synapse Analytics to aggregate and transform data from various sources into a central data warehouse, and leverage Power BI to create interactive reports and dashboards for data analysis and visualization.

Scenario:

Q104: Question: How can I implement a serverless predictive maintenance solution for IoT devices in Azure?

Answer: Azure IoT Hub, Azure Machine Learning, and Azure Functions can be used together to implement a serverless predictive maintenance solution for IoT devices in Azure. Azure IoT Hub is a managed service that enables secure and scalable communication between devices and the cloud. Azure Machine Learning allows you to build, deploy, and manage machine learning models. Azure Functions provides serverless compute resources that can be triggered by events. You can use Azure IoT Hub to ingest telemetry data from IoT devices, use Azure Machine Learning to train predictive maintenance models, and leverage Azure Functions for real-time analysis and triggering of maintenance alerts based on the predictive models.

Scenario:

Q105: Question: How can I implement a serverless data cataloging and discovery solution in Azure?

Answer: Azure Purview and Azure Logic Apps can be used together to implement a serverless data cataloging and discovery solution in Azure. Azure Purview is a unified data governance service that provides a holistic view of your data assets and their metadata. Azure Logic Apps provides a visual workflow designer that allows you to create automated workflows for integrating and orchestrating services. You can use Azure Logic Apps to automate the process of cataloging data assets in Azure Purview, extract metadata from various sources, and enable easy discovery and search capabilities for your data assets.

AZURE INTERVIEW QUESTIONS

Scenario:

Q106: Question: How can I implement a serverless anomaly detection solution in Azure?

Answer: Azure Machine Learning and Azure Stream Analytics can be used together to implement a serverless anomaly detection solution in Azure. Azure Machine Learning allows you to build, deploy, and manage machine learning models. Azure Stream Analytics is a real-time analytics service that allows you to process and analyze streaming data from various sources. You can use Azure Stream Analytics to ingest and process real-time data, and leverage Azure Machine Learning to detect anomalies in the data based on trained models and statistical analysis.

Scenario:

Q107: Question: How can I implement a serverless data transformation and enrichment solution in Azure?

Answer: Azure Data Factory and Azure Databricks can be used together to implement a serverless data transformation and enrichment solution in Azure. Azure Data Factory is a cloud-based data integration service that allows you to create data-driven workflows for orchestrating and automating data movement and transformation. Azure Databricks is an Apache Spark-based analytics platform that provides a collaborative environment for big data analytics and machine learning. You can use Azure Data Factory to orchestrate the process of extracting data from the source, applying transformations and enrichment using Azure Databricks, and loading the transformed data into the target destination.

Scenario:

Q108: Question: How can I implement a serverless recommendation system for e-commerce in Azure?

Answer: Azure Personalizer and Azure Functions can be used together to implement a serverless recommendation system for e-commerce in Azure. Azure Personalizer is a service that uses reinforcement learning to provide personalized recommendations. Azure Functions provides serverless compute resources that can be triggered by events. You can use Azure Functions to build custom logic that integrates with Azure Personalizer and processes user behavior data in real-time, generating personalized recommendations for products or content based on the user's preferences and past interactions.

Scenario:

Q109: Question: How can I implement a serverless data validation and cleansing solution in Azure?

Answer: Azure Data Factory and Azure Databricks can be used

together to implement a serverless data validation and cleansing solution in Azure. Azure Data Factory is a cloud-based data integration service that allows you to create data-driven workflows for orchestrating and automating data movement and transformation. Azure Databricks is an Apache Spark-based analytics platform that provides a collaborative environment for big data analytics and machine learning. You can use Azure Data Factory to orchestrate the process of extracting data from the source, performing validation and cleansing tasks using Azure Databricks, and loading the clean data into the target destination.

Scenario:

Q110: Question: How can I implement a serverless natural language processing (NLP) solution in Azure?

Answer: Azure Cognitive Services, specifically Text Analytics and Azure Functions, can be used together to implement a serverless natural language processing (NLP) solution in Azure. Text Analytics provides capabilities for sentiment analysis, key phrase extraction, and entity recognition. Azure Functions provides serverless compute resources that can be triggered by events. You can use Azure Functions to build custom logic that integrates with Text Analytics and processes text data in real-time, extracting insights, sentiment, and key information from the text.

These answers should provide you with further insights into

different scenarios and their corresponding solutions in Azure. Remember to consider your specific needs and consult Azure documentation for detailed guidance and best practices.

Scenario:

Q111: Question: How can I implement a serverless data streaming and analytics solution in Azure?

Answer: Azure Event Hubs and Azure Stream Analytics can be used together to implement a serverless data streaming and analytics solution in Azure. Azure Event Hubs is a scalable event streaming platform that can handle millions of events per second. Azure Stream Analytics is a real-time analytics service that allows you to process and analyze streaming data from various sources. You can use Azure Event Hubs to ingest and store the streaming data, and leverage Azure Stream Analytics to process and analyze the data in real-time for insights, aggregations, or filtering.

Scenario:

Q112: Question: How can I implement a serverless geospatial analysis solution in Azure?

Answer: Azure Maps and Azure Functions can be used together to implement a serverless geospatial analysis solution in Azure. Azure Maps is a set of geospatial services that provide mapping, routing, and spatial analysis capabilities. Azure Functions provides serverless compute resources that can be triggered by events. You can use Azure Functions to build custom logic that integrates with Azure Maps and performs geospatial analysis tasks, such as proximity search, routing optimization, or geofencing based on specific events or user inputs.

Scenario:

Q113: Question: How can I implement a serverless data archiving and retention solution in Azure?

Answer: Azure Blob Storage and Azure Logic Apps can be used together to implement a serverless data archiving and retention solution in Azure. Azure Blob Storage is a scalable and cost-effective storage service that allows you to store and retrieve unstructured data, such as files or backups. Azure Logic Apps provides a visual workflow designer that allows you to create automated workflows for integrating and orchestrating services. You can use Azure Logic Apps to automate the process of archiving and retaining data in Azure Blob Storage based on specific triggers or schedule, ensuring long-term storage and compliance with retention policies.

Scenario:

Q114: Question: How can I implement a serverless data encryption and decryption solution in Azure?

Answer: Azure Key Vault and Azure Functions can be used together to implement a serverless data encryption and decryption solution in Azure. Azure Key Vault is a cloud service that allows you to securely store and manage cryptographic keys, certificates, and secrets. Azure Functions provides serverless compute resources that can be triggered by events. You can use Azure Functions to build custom logic that integrates with Azure Key Vault and performs encryption and decryption tasks for sensitive data, ensuring secure storage and transmission of data.

Scenario:

Q115: Question: How can I implement a serverless chatbot solution in Azure?

Answer: Azure Bot Service and Azure Cognitive Services, specifically Language Understanding (LUIS) and Text Analytics, can be used together to implement a serverless chatbot solution in Azure. Azure Bot Service is a platform for building, deploying, and managing chatbots. LUIS provides natural language understanding capabilities to enable the chatbot to understand user intents and entities. Text Analytics can be used to extract insights and sentiment from user messages. You can use Azure Bot Service to build and deploy the chatbot, integrate LUIS for natural language understanding, and leverage Text Analytics for sentiment analysis or other text analysis tasks within the chatbot.

AZURE INTERVIEW QUESTIONS

Scenario:

Q116: Question: How can I implement a serverless data pipeline for real-time analytics in Azure?

Answer: Azure Event Hubs, Azure Stream Analytics, and Azure Functions can be used together to implement a serverless data pipeline for real-time analytics in Azure. Azure Event Hubs is a scalable event streaming platform for ingesting and storing data in real-time. Azure Stream Analytics is a real-time analytics service that allows you to process and analyze streaming data from various sources. Azure Functions provides serverless compute resources that can be triggered by events. You can use Azure Event Hubs to ingest and store the streaming data, leverage Azure Stream Analytics to perform real-time analytics on the data, and use Azure Functions for further processing or triggering downstream actions based on the analytics results.

Scenario:

Q117: Question: How can I implement a serverless image recognition solution in Azure?

Answer: Azure Cognitive Services, specifically Computer Vision and Azure Functions, can be used together to implement a serverless image recognition solution in Azure. Computer Vision provides capabilities for image analysis, including object recognition, text extraction, and image classification. Azure Functions provides serverless compute resources that can be triggered by events. You can use Azure Functions to build custom logic that integrates with Computer Vision and processes images in real-time, extracting relevant information or triggering actions based on the analysis results.

Scenario:

Q118: Question: How can I implement a serverless data backup and disaster recovery solution for virtual machines in Azure?

Answer: Azure Backup and Azure Site Recovery can be used together to implement a serverless data backup and disaster recovery solution for virtual machines in Azure. Azure Backup is a scalable and secure service that allows you to back up data from virtual machines, databases, and files. Azure Site Recovery is a disaster recovery service that enables replication and recovery of virtual machines and physical servers. You can use Azure Backup to schedule and automate backups of virtual machine data, and leverage Azure Site Recovery for replicating and recovering virtual machines in the event of a disaster or outage.

Scenario:

Q119: Question: How can I implement a serverless data warehousing solution in Azure?

Answer: Azure Synapse Analytics and Azure Data Factory can be used together to implement a serverless data warehousing solution in Azure. Azure Synapse Analytics is an analytics service that combines enterprise data warehousing, big data integration, and data integration. Azure Data Factory is a cloud-based data integration service that allows you to create data-driven workflows for orchestrating and automating data movement and transformation. You can use Azure Data Factory to orchestrate the process of extracting data from various sources, transforming and loading the data into Azure Synapse Analytics for analysis, and leveraging the serverless capabilities of Azure Synapse Analytics for on-demand scaling and cost efficiency.

Scenario:

Q120: Question: How can I implement a serverless data governance and compliance solution in Azure?

Answer: Azure Purview and Azure Policy can be used together to implement a serverless data governance and compliance solution in Azure. Azure Purview is a unified data governance service that provides a holistic view of your data assets and their metadata, enabling data discovery, classification, and lineage. Azure Policy is a service for creating and enforcing policy-based rules and regulations for resources in Azure. You can use Azure Purview to catalog and govern your data assets, and leverage Azure Policy to enforce data governance policies, such as access control, data retention, or compliance requirements, across your Azure environment.

Scenario:

Q121: Question: How can I implement a serverless data integration solution with multiple data sources in Azure?

Answer: Azure Data Factory and Azure Logic Apps can be used together to implement a serverless data integration solution with multiple data sources in Azure. Azure Data Factory is a cloud-based data integration service that allows you to create data-driven workflows for orchestrating and automating data movement and transformation. Azure Logic Apps provides a visual workflow designer that allows you to create automated workflows for integrating and orchestrating services. You can use Azure Data Factory to orchestrate the process of extracting data from multiple sources, transforming the data, and loading it into the target destination. Azure Logic Apps can be used to integrate with various services and trigger data integration workflows based on specific events or schedules.

Scenario:

Q122: Question: How can I implement a serverless document processing solution in Azure?

Answer: Azure Form Recognizer, Azure Blob Storage, and Azure

Functions can be used together to implement a serverless document processing solution in Azure. Azure Form Recognizer is a service that uses machine learning to extract structured data from forms and documents. Azure Blob Storage is a scalable and cost-effective storage service for storing unstructured data. Azure Functions provides serverless compute resources that can be triggered by events. You can use Azure Functions to build custom logic that integrates with Azure Form Recognizer and processes documents in real-time, extracting structured data from the documents and storing it in Azure Blob Storage for further analysis or retrieval.

Scenario:

Q123: Question: How can I implement a serverless IoT data ingestion and processing solution in Azure?

Answer: Azure IoT Hub, Azure Stream Analytics, and Azure Functions can be used together to implement a serverless IoT data ingestion and processing solution in Azure. Azure IoT Hub is a managed service that enables secure and scalable communication between devices and the cloud. Azure Stream Analytics is a real-time analytics service that allows you to process and analyze streaming data from various sources. Azure Functions provides serverless compute resources that can be triggered by events. You can use Azure IoT Hub to ingest telemetry data from IoT devices, leverage Azure Stream Analytics to process and analyze the data in real-time, and use Azure Functions for further processing, transformation, or triggering of actions based on the analyzed data.

Scenario:

Q124: Question: How can I implement a serverless video processing and analysis solution in Azure?

Answer: Azure Media Services, Azure Cognitive Services (Video Indexer), and Azure Functions can be used together to implement a serverless video processing and analysis solution in Azure. Azure Media Services is a scalable and secure platform for encoding, streaming, and delivering video content. Azure Cognitive Services, specifically Video Indexer, provides AI capabilities for extracting insights and metadata from video content. Azure Functions provides serverless compute resources that can be triggered by events. You can use Azure Media Services to upload and process video content, leverage Azure Cognitive Services for analyzing the video content and extracting insights, and use Azure Functions for further processing or triggering of actions based on the video analysis results.

Scenario:

Q125: Question: How can I implement a serverless data synchronization solution between on-premises and Azure databases?

Answer: Azure Hybrid Connections and Azure Data Sync can be

used together to implement a serverless data synchronization solution between on-premises and Azure databases. Azure Hybrid Connections allows you to securely access on-premises resources from Azure without requiring any changes to the network infrastructure. Azure Data Sync is a service that enables bi-directional data synchronization between multiple Azure SQL databases and on-premises SQL Server databases. You can use Azure Hybrid Connections to establish connectivity between your on-premises databases and Azure, and leverage Azure Data Sync to configure synchronization groups and rules for keeping the data synchronized between the on-premises and Azure databases.

Scenario:

Q126: Question: How can I implement a serverless data transformation and enrichment solution in Azure?

Answer: Azure Data Factory, Azure Databricks, and Azure Functions can be used together to implement a serverless data transformation and enrichment solution in Azure. Azure Data Factory is a cloud-based data integration service that allows you to create data-driven workflows for orchestrating and automating data movement and transformation. Azure Databricks is an analytics service that provides a collaborative environment for big data and machine learning workloads. Azure Functions provides serverless compute resources that can be triggered by events. You can use Azure Data Factory to orchestrate the process of extracting data, performing transformations and enrichments using Azure Databricks, and loading the transformed data into the target destination. Azure Functions can be used to integrate with the workflow and perform additional data processing tasks if needed.

Scenario:

Q127: Question: How can I implement a serverless data caching solution in Azure?

Answer: Azure Cache for Redis and Azure Functions can be used together to implement a serverless data caching solution in Azure. Azure Cache for Redis is a fully managed, in-memory caching service that allows you to store and retrieve data with low latency. Azure Functions provides serverless compute resources that can be triggered by events. You can use Azure Functions to build custom logic that integrates with Azure Cache for Redis and performs caching operations based on specific events or triggers. This allows you to cache frequently accessed data and improve the performance and responsiveness of your applications.

Scenario:

Q128: Question: How can I implement a serverless anomaly detection solution in Azure?

Answer: Azure Time Series Insights and Azure Functions can be used together to implement a serverless anomaly detection solution in Azure. Azure Time Series Insights is a fully managed service that allows you to store, visualize, and analyze time series data. Azure Functions provides serverless compute resources that can be triggered by events. You can use Azure Functions to build custom logic that integrates with Azure Time Series Insights and performs anomaly detection algorithms on the time series data. This enables you to identify and alert on anomalous patterns or behaviors in your data, allowing for proactive monitoring and troubleshooting.

Scenario:

Q129: Question: How can I implement a serverless sentiment analysis solution in Azure?

Answer: Azure Cognitive Services, specifically Text Analytics and Azure Functions, can be used together to implement a serverless sentiment analysis solution in Azure. Text Analytics provides natural language processing capabilities for sentiment analysis, key phrase extraction, and language detection. Azure Functions provides serverless compute resources that can be triggered by events. You can use Azure Functions to build custom logic that integrates with Text Analytics and performs sentiment analysis on text inputs. This allows you to analyze the sentiment of customer feedback, social media posts, or any other text data, and gain insights into the overall sentiment trends.

Scenario:

Q130: Question: How can I implement a serverless data visualization solution in Azure?

Answer: Azure Power BI and Azure Functions can be used together to implement a serverless data visualization solution in Azure. Azure Power BI is a business analytics service that provides interactive visualizations and business intelligence capabilities. Azure Functions provides serverless compute resources that can be triggered by events. You can use Azure Functions to build custom logic that integrates with Azure Power BI and retrieves data from various sources, performs data transformations if needed, and feeds the data into Power BI for visualization and interactive reporting. This enables you to create real-time or scheduled data dashboards and visualizations based on your specific business needs.

Scenario:

Q131: Question: How can I implement a serverless data archival solution in Azure?

Answer: Azure Blob Storage, Azure Logic Apps, and Azure Functions can be used together to implement a serverless data archival solution in Azure. Azure Blob Storage is a scalable and cost-effective storage service for storing unstructured data. Azure Logic Apps provides a visual workflow designer that allows you to create automated workflows for integrating and orchestrating services. Azure Functions provides serverless compute resources that can be triggered by events. You can use Azure Logic Apps to create a workflow that triggers Azure Functions to move or copy data from hot or cool storage tiers to an archival tier in Azure Blob Storage based on specific criteria, such as data age or usage patterns. This allows you to optimize storage costs by automatically moving infrequently accessed data to a more cost-effective storage tier for long-term retention.

Scenario:

Q132: Question: How can I implement a serverless chatbot solution in Azure?

Answer: Azure Bot Service, Azure Cognitive Services (Language Understanding), and Azure Functions can be used together to implement a serverless chatbot solution in Azure. Azure Bot Service is a fully managed service for building, deploying, and managing chatbots. Azure Cognitive Services, specifically Language Understanding (LUIS), provides natural language processing capabilities for understanding user intents and entities. Azure Functions provides serverless compute resources that can be triggered by events. You can use Azure Bot Service to create and deploy your chatbot, leverage Azure Cognitive Services (LUIS) to understand and interpret user messages, and use Azure Functions to build custom logic for processing user requests, retrieving information from external systems, or triggering actions based on the chatbot interactions.

Scenario:

Q133: Question: How can I implement a serverless recommendation engine in Azure?

Answer: Azure Machine Learning, Azure Databricks, and Azure Functions can be used together to implement a serverless recommendation engine in Azure. Azure Machine Learning is a cloud-based service for building, training, and deploying machine learning models. Azure Databricks is an analytics service that provides a collaborative environment for big data and machine learning workloads. Azure Functions provides serverless compute resources that can be triggered by events. You can use Azure Databricks to train and refine your recommendation models, leverage Azure Machine Learning for model deployment and serving, and use Azure Functions to build custom logic for recommending items or generating personalized recommendations based on user behavior and preferences.

Scenario:

Q134: Question: How can I implement a serverless event-driven architecture in Azure?

Answer: Azure Event Grid, Azure Functions, and Azure Logic Apps can be used together to implement a serverless event-driven architecture in Azure. Azure Event Grid is a fully managed event

AZURE INTERVIEW QUESTIONS

routing service that allows you to react to events from various sources. Azure Functions provides serverless compute resources that can be triggered by events. Azure Logic Apps provides a visual workflow designer that allows you to create automated workflows for integrating and orchestrating services. You can use Azure Event Grid to route events to Azure Functions or Azure Logic Apps based on specific conditions or filters, trigger serverless functions or workflows to process the events, and perform actions such as sending notifications, updating data, or triggering other business processes based on the event-driven architecture.

Scenario:

Q135: Question: How can I implement a serverless data anonymization solution in Azure?

Answer: Azure Data Factory, Azure Databricks, and Azure Functions can be used together to implement a serverless data anonymization solution in Azure. Azure Data Factory is a cloud-based data integration service that allows you to create data-driven workflows for orchestrating and automating data movement and transformation. Azure Databricks is an analytics service that provides a collaborative environment for big data and machine learning workloads.

Scenario:

Q136: Question: How can I implement a serverless image

recognition solution in Azure?

Answer: Azure Cognitive Services (Computer Vision), Azure Blob Storage, and Azure Functions can be used together to implement a serverless image recognition solution in Azure. Azure Cognitive Services (Computer Vision) provides AI capabilities for analyzing images and extracting information from them. Azure Blob Storage is a scalable and cost-effective storage service for storing unstructured data. Azure Functions provides serverless compute resources that can be triggered by events. You can use Azure Functions to build custom logic that integrates with Azure Cognitive Services (Computer Vision) and processes images stored in Azure Blob Storage, extracting information such as objects, faces, or text from the images. This allows you to automate image recognition tasks and gain insights from your image data.

Scenario:

Q137: Question: How can I implement a serverless data backup solution in Azure?

Answer: Azure Backup and Azure Functions can be used together to implement a serverless data backup solution in Azure. Azure Backup is a scalable and cost-effective backup service that allows you to protect your data and applications in the cloud and on-premises. Azure Functions provides serverless compute resources that can be triggered by events. You can use Azure Functions to build custom logic that integrates with Azure Backup and triggers backup operations based on specific events or schedules. This allows you to automate the backup process for your data and ensure its availability and recoverability in case of data loss or system failures.

Scenario:

Q138: Question: How can I implement a serverless fraud detection solution in Azure?

Answer: Azure Machine Learning, Azure Stream Analytics, and Azure Functions can be used together to implement a serverless fraud detection solution in Azure. Azure Machine Learning is a cloud-based service for building, training, and deploying machine learning models. Azure Stream Analytics is a real-time analytics service that allows you to process and analyze streaming data from various sources. Azure Functions provides serverless compute resources that can be triggered by events. You can use Azure Stream Analytics to ingest and analyze streaming data, leverage Azure Machine Learning to build and deploy fraud detection models, and use Azure Functions to perform real-time scoring and trigger actions based on detected fraud patterns, such as generating alerts or blocking transactions.

Scenario:

Q139: Question: How can I implement a serverless data

encryption solution in Azure?

Answer: Azure Key Vault, Azure Functions, and Azure Blob Storage can be used together to implement a serverless data encryption solution in Azure. Azure Key Vault is a cloud-based service that allows you to safeguard cryptographic keys and secrets used by your applications. Azure Functions provides serverless compute resources that can be triggered by events. Azure Blob Storage is a scalable and cost-effective storage service for storing unstructured data. You can use Azure Key Vault to store and manage encryption keys, leverage Azure Functions to build custom logic that integrates with Azure Key Vault and performs encryption and decryption operations on data, and store the encrypted data in Azure Blob Storage. This ensures that your data is protected and can only be accessed by authorized users or processes.

Scenario:

Q140: Question: How can I implement a serverless data streaming solution in Azure?

Answer: Azure Event Hubs, Azure Stream Analytics, and Azure Functions can be used together to implement a serverless data streaming solution in Azure. Azure Event Hubs is a scalable and event ingestion service that allows you to collect and process large volumes of streaming data from various sources. Azure Stream Analytics is a real-time analytics service that allows you to process and analyze streaming data from Azure Event Hubs and other sources. Azure Functions provides serverless compute resources that can be triggered by events. You can use Azure Event Hubs to ingest and collect streaming data, leverage Azure Stream Analytics to process and analyze the data in real-time, and use Azure Functions to trigger actions or perform additional data processing based on the streaming data. This enables you to build real-time data processing and analytics solutions, such as real-time monitoring, IoT data processing, or fraud detection.

Scenario:

Q141: Question: How can I implement a serverless data synchronization solution in Azure?

Answer: Azure Data Factory, Azure SQL Database, and Azure Functions can be used together to implement a serverless data synchronization solution in Azure. Azure Data Factory is a cloud-based data integration service that allows you to create data-driven workflows for orchestrating and automating data movement and transformation. Azure SQL Database is a fully managed relational database service in Azure. Azure Functions provides serverless compute resources that can be triggered by events. You can use Azure Data Factory to orchestrate the process of synchronizing data between different data sources, such as on-premises databases and Azure SQL Database, using built-in connectors and data integration capabilities. Azure Functions can be used to perform custom data transformations or to trigger synchronization processes based on specific events or schedules.

Scenario:

Q142: Question: How can I implement a serverless log analytics solution in Azure?

Answer: Azure Log Analytics, Azure Monitor, and Azure Functions can be used together to implement a serverless log analytics solution in Azure. Azure Log Analytics is a service that collects and analyzes log and telemetry data from various sources. Azure Monitor provides monitoring and alerting capabilities for Azure resources and applications. Azure Functions provides serverless compute resources that can be triggered by events. You can use Azure Log Analytics to collect and store log data from different sources, leverage Azure Monitor to monitor and analyze the log data for insights and anomalies, and use Azure Functions to build custom logic that integrates with Log Analytics and performs actions based on specific log events, such as sending notifications, triggering automated responses, or generating reports.

Scenario:

Q143: Question: How can I implement a serverless geospatial analysis solution in Azure?

Answer: Azure Maps, Azure Spatial Anchors, and Azure Functions can be used together to implement a serverless geospatial analysis solution in Azure. Azure Maps is a set of location-based services that provides mapping, geocoding, routing, and other geospatial capabilities. Azure Spatial Anchors is a mixed reality service that allows you to create and manage spatial anchors for augmented reality (AR) experiences. Azure Functions provides serverless compute resources that can be triggered by events. You can use Azure Functions to build custom logic that integrates with Azure Maps and Azure Spatial Anchors, perform geospatial analysis on location data, and trigger actions or notifications based on specific geospatial events, such as proximity alerts, geofencing, or route optimization.

Scenario:

Q144: Question: How can I implement a serverless data replication solution in Azure?

Answer: Azure Cosmos DB, Azure Data Factory, and Azure Functions can be used together to implement a serverless data replication solution in Azure. Azure Cosmos DB is a globally distributed, multi-model database service. Azure Data Factory is a cloud-based data integration service that allows you to create data-driven workflows for orchestrating and automating data movement and transformation. Azure Functions provides serverless compute resources that can be triggered by events. You can use Azure Data

Factory to orchestrate the process of replicating data from one Azure Cosmos DB account to another, using built-in connectors and data integration capabilities. Azure Functions can be used to perform custom data transformations or to trigger replication processes based on specific events or schedules.

Scenario:

Q145: Question: How can I implement a serverless video processing solution in Azure?

Answer: Azure Media Services, Azure Functions, and Azure Storage can be used together to implement a serverless video processing solution in Azure. Azure Media Services is a cloud-based media processing and streaming platform. Azure Functions provides serverless compute resources that can be triggered by events. Azure Storage is a scalable and cost-effective storage service for storing unstructured data. You can use Azure Media Services to ingest, encode, and process video files, leverage Azure Functions to build custom logic that integrates with Azure Media Services and performs additional video processing or analysis tasks, and store the processed videos in Azure Storage for further use or streaming.

Scenario:

Q146: Question: How can I implement a serverless data warehousing solution in Azure?

Answer: Azure Synapse Analytics (formerly SQL Data Warehouse), Azure Data Factory, and Azure Functions can be used together to implement a serverless data warehousing solution in Azure. Azure Synapse Analytics is an analytics service that provides a fully managed and scalable data warehousing solution. Azure Data Factory is a cloud-based data integration service that allows you to create data-driven workflows for orchestrating and automating data movement and transformation. Azure Functions provides serverless compute resources that can be triggered by events. You can use Azure Data Factory to orchestrate the process of extracting, transforming, and loading data into Azure Synapse Analytics, leverage Azure Functions to perform custom data transformations or trigger ETL processes, and utilize Azure Synapse Analytics to store and analyze large volumes of structured and unstructured data for business intelligence and reporting purposes.

Scenario:

Q147: Question: How can I implement a serverless IoT solution in Azure?

Answer: Azure IoT Hub, Azure Functions, and Azure Stream Analytics can be used together to implement a serverless IoT solution in Azure. Azure IoT Hub is a fully managed service that enables bi-directional communication between IoT devices and the cloud. Azure Functions provides serverless compute resources that can be triggered by events. Azure Stream Analytics is a real-time analytics service that allows you to process and analyze streaming data from IoT devices and other sources. You can use Azure IoT Hub to connect and manage your IoT devices, leverage Azure Functions to build custom logic that integrates with IoT Hub and performs actions based on device telemetry or events, and use Azure Stream Analytics to process and gain insights from the streaming data generated by the IoT devices.

Scenario:

Q148: Question: How can I implement a serverless document processing solution in Azure?

Answer: Azure Cognitive Services (Form Recognizer), Azure Functions, and Azure Blob Storage can be used together to implement a serverless document processing solution in Azure. Azure Cognitive Services (Form Recognizer) is an AI service that automates the extraction of information from forms and documents. Azure Functions provides serverless compute resources that can be triggered by events. Azure Blob Storage is a scalable and cost-effective storage service for storing unstructured data. You can use Azure Functions to build custom logic that integrates with Azure Cognitive Services (Form Recognizer) and processes documents stored in Azure Blob Storage, extracting structured data such as key-value pairs or tables from the documents. This enables you to automate document processing tasks, such as invoice processing, expense report extraction, or contract analysis.

AZURE INTERVIEW QUESTIONS

Scenario:

Q149: Question: How can I implement a serverless data integration solution in Azure?

Answer: Azure Logic Apps, Azure Data Factory, and Azure Functions can be used together to implement a serverless data integration solution in Azure. Azure Logic Apps provides a visual workflow designer that allows you to create automated workflows for integrating and orchestrating services. Azure Data Factory is a cloud-based data integration service that allows you to create data-driven workflows for orchestrating and automating data movement and transformation. Azure Functions provides serverless compute resources that can be triggered by events. You can use Azure Logic Apps to create workflows that integrate with various services and systems, leverage Azure Data Factory to orchestrate the data integration processes, and use Azure Functions to build custom logic or perform additional data processing tasks within the workflows. This enables you to automate and streamline data integration across different applications and systems.

Scenario:

Q150: Question: How can I implement a serverless machine learning inference solution in Azure?

Answer: Azure Machine Learning, Azure Functions, and Azure

Kubernetes Service (AKS) can be used together to implement a serverless machine learning inference solution in Azure. Azure Machine Learning is a cloud-based service for building, training, and deploying machine learning models. Azure Functions provides serverless compute resources that can be triggered by events. Azure Kubernetes Service (AKS) is a managed container orchestration service that simplifies the deployment and management of containerized applications. You can use Azure Machine Learning to train and deploy your machine learning models, leverage Azure Functions to build custom logic that integrates with the deployed models and performs inference tasks based on specific events or requests, and utilize Azure Kubernetes Service (AKS) to scale and manage the containerized inference workload efficiently.

Scenario:

Q151: Question: How can I implement a serverless data analytics solution in Azure?

Answer: Azure Synapse Analytics, Azure Data Lake Storage, and Azure Functions can be used together to implement a serverless data analytics solution in Azure. Azure Synapse Analytics provides a unified analytics platform that combines big data and data warehousing capabilities. Azure Data Lake Storage is a scalable and secure data lake solution for big data analytics. Azure Functions provides serverless compute resources that can be triggered by events. You can use Azure Synapse Analytics to process and analyze large volumes of structured and unstructured data, leverage Azure Data Lake Storage as a data repository for storing and accessing the data, and use Azure Functions to build custom logic that integrates with Synapse Analytics and performs additional data processing tasks or triggers analytics workflows based on specific events or schedules.

Scenario:

Q152: Question: How can I implement a serverless chatbot solution in Azure?

Answer: Azure Bot Service, Azure Functions, and Azure Cognitive Services (Language Understanding) can be used together to implement a serverless chatbot solution in Azure. Azure Bot Service provides a platform for building and deploying chatbots. Azure Functions provides serverless compute resources that can be triggered by events. Azure Cognitive Services (Language Understanding) enables the chatbot to understand and interpret user input. You can use Azure Bot Service to design and develop your chatbot, leverage Azure Functions to build custom logic and integrate with external systems or APIs, and use Azure Cognitive Services (Language Understanding) to enhance the natural language processing capabilities of the chatbot. This allows you to create intelligent chatbots that can understand and respond to user queries and perform tasks or provide information in a conversational manner.

Scenario:

Q153: Question: How can I implement a serverless data archival solution in Azure?

Answer: Azure Blob Storage, Azure Data Factory, and Azure Functions can be used together to implement a serverless data archival solution in Azure. Azure Blob Storage is a scalable and cost-effective storage service for storing unstructured data. Azure Data Factory is a cloud-based data integration service that allows you to create data-driven workflows for orchestrating and automating data movement and transformation. Azure Functions provides serverless compute resources that can be triggered by events. You can use Azure Data Factory to orchestrate the process of moving and archiving data from a primary storage location to Azure Blob Storage, leverage Azure Functions to perform custom data transformations or trigger archival processes based on specific events or schedules, and utilize Azure Blob Storage for long-term storage and retention of archived data.

Scenario:

Q154: Question: How can I implement a serverless media transcoding solution in Azure?

Answer: Azure Media Services, Azure Functions, and Azure Blob Storage can be used together to implement a serverless media transcoding solution in Azure. Azure Media Services is a cloud-based media processing and streaming platform. Azure Functions provides serverless compute resources that can be triggered by events. Azure Blob Storage is a scalable and cost-effective storage service for storing unstructured data. You can use Azure Media Services to ingest and process media files, leverage Azure Functions to build custom logic that integrates with Media Services and performs additional media processing tasks, such as transcoding or format conversion, and use Azure Blob Storage to store the processed media files for further use or streaming.

Scenario:

Q155: Question: How can I implement a serverless data governance solution in Azure?

Answer: Azure Purview, Azure Data Catalog, and Azure Functions can be used together to implement a serverless data governance solution in Azure. Azure Purview is a unified data governance service that helps you discover, understand, and manage your data. Azure Data Catalog is a fully managed service for registering, discovering, and managing data assets. Azure Functions provides serverless compute resources that can be triggered by events.

Scenario:

Q156: Question: How can I implement a serverless data streaming solution in Azure?

Answer: Azure Event Hubs, Azure Functions, and Azure Stream Analytics can be used together to implement a serverless data streaming solution in Azure. Azure Event Hubs is a highly scalable and event ingestion service. Azure Functions provides serverless compute resources that can be triggered by events. Azure Stream Analytics is a real-time analytics service that allows you to process and analyze streaming data. You can use Azure Event Hubs to ingest and buffer large volumes of streaming data, leverage Azure Functions to build custom logic that integrates with Event Hubs and performs additional data processing or transformation, and use Azure Stream Analytics to process and gain insights from the streaming data in real-time.

Scenario:

Q157: Question: How can I implement a serverless image recognition solution in Azure?

Answer: Azure Cognitive Services (Computer Vision), Azure Functions, and Azure Blob Storage can be used together to implement a serverless image recognition solution in Azure. Azure Cognitive Services (Computer Vision) is an AI service that provides image recognition capabilities. Azure Functions provides serverless compute resources that can be triggered by events. Azure Blob Storage is a scalable and cost-effective storage service for storing unstructured data. You can use Azure Cognitive Services

(Computer Vision) to analyze and recognize the content of images, leverage Azure Functions to build custom logic that integrates with Computer Vision and performs additional image processing or analysis tasks, and use Azure Blob Storage to store and retrieve the images for processing.

Scenario:

Q158: Question: How can I implement a serverless data backup solution in Azure?

Answer: Azure Backup, Azure Functions, and Azure Storage can be used together to implement a serverless data backup solution in Azure. Azure Backup is a scalable and cost-effective data protection service. Azure Functions provides serverless compute resources that can be triggered by events. Azure Storage is a durable and highly available storage service in Azure. You can use Azure Backup to create and manage backup policies for your data, leverage Azure Functions to build custom logic that integrates with Azure Backup and performs additional backup-related tasks, such as notifications or data validation, and use Azure Storage to store the backup data securely.

Scenario:

Q159: Question: How can I implement a serverless data validation solution in Azure?

Answer: Azure Data Factory, Azure Functions, and Azure SQL Database can be used together to implement a serverless data validation solution in Azure. Azure Data Factory is a cloud-based data integration service that allows you to create data-driven workflows for orchestrating and automating data movement and transformation. Azure Functions provides serverless compute resources that can be triggered by events. Azure SQL Database is a fully managed relational database service in Azure. You can use Azure Data Factory to orchestrate the process of moving and validating data, leverage Azure Functions to build custom logic that integrates with Data Factory and performs data validation tasks based on specific events or schedules, and use Azure SQL Database to store and analyze the validated data.

Scenario:

Q160: Question: How can I implement a serverless event-driven architecture in Azure?

Answer: Azure Event Grid, Azure Functions, and Azure Service Bus can be used together to implement a serverless event-driven architecture in Azure. Azure Event Grid is a fully managed event routing service. Azure Functions provides serverless compute resources that can be triggered by events. Azure Service Bus is a messaging service for connecting distributed systems. You can use Azure Event Grid to route and process events from various sources, leverage Azure Functions to build custom logic that integrates with

AZURE INTERVIEW QUESTIONS

Event Grid and performs actions based on specific events or event patterns, and use Azure Service Bus to decouple components and enable asynchronous communication between different parts of your application or system.

AZURE INTERVIEW QUESTIONS AND ANSWERS

Q161: What are the key components of Azure architecture?
Answer: The key components of Azure architecture include Azure Virtual Machines, Azure Storage, Azure App Service, Azure Functions, Azure SQL Database, Azure Virtual Network, Azure Load Balancer, and Azure Active Directory.

Q162: How does Azure differ from AWS?
Answer: Azure and AWS are both cloud computing platforms, but they differ in terms of services offered, pricing models, and market presence. Azure has a strong integration with Microsoft technologies and offers services like Azure Active Directory, Azure Functions, and Azure SQL Database. AWS, on the other hand, has a broader range of services and is known for its mature infrastructure and scalability options.

Q163: What is Azure DevOps and how does it facilitate the DevOps process?
Answer: Azure DevOps is a set of development tools and services that facilitate the DevOps process, including continuous integration, continuous delivery, and application monitoring. It includes services like Azure Pipelines for automating build and release processes, Azure Boards for project management, Azure Repos for version control, and Azure Test Plans for testing and

quality assurance.

Q164: How can you secure Azure resources and data?

Answer: Azure provides several security measures to secure resources and data, including network security groups, virtual network service endpoints, Azure Firewall, Azure DDoS Protection, Azure Active Directory for identity and access management, Azure Security Center for threat detection and monitoring, and Azure Key Vault for storing and managing cryptographic keys and secrets.

Q165: What is Azure Functions and how can they be used?

Answer: Azure Functions is a serverless compute service that allows you to run event-driven code in the cloud. Functions can be used for various purposes, such as responding to HTTP requests, processing messages from Azure Service Bus or Azure Event Grid, triggering actions based on changes in Azure Storage, or running scheduled tasks. They enable you to focus on writing code without worrying about infrastructure management.

Q166: What is Azure Cosmos DB and when should it be used?

Answer: Azure Cosmos DB is a globally distributed, multi-model database service. It offers high scalability, low latency, and guaranteed performance. Cosmos DB can be used for applications that require low-latency data access, global distribution, and support for multiple data models such as SQL, MongoDB, Cassandra, Gremlin, and Table API.

Q167: How can you optimize costs in Azure?

Answer: To optimize costs in Azure, you can use services like Azure Cost Management and Billing to monitor and analyze your usage, right-size virtual machines and other resources to match workload requirements, leverage Azure Reserved VM Instances and Azure Hybrid Benefit for cost savings, use Azure Spot Virtual Machines for non-critical workloads, and implement automation and policies to manage resource allocation and usage.

Q168: What is Azure Kubernetes Service (AKS) and how does it simplify container orchestration?

Answer: Azure Kubernetes Service (AKS) is a managed container orchestration service that simplifies the deployment, management, and scaling of containerized applications using Kubernetes. AKS takes care of the underlying infrastructure, including the provisioning of nodes, and provides features like automatic scaling, monitoring, and integration with Azure services.

Q169: How can you ensure high availability and disaster recovery in Azure?

Answer: To ensure high availability and disaster recovery in Azure, you can use features like Availability Sets or Availability Zones for fault tolerance, implement load balancing and auto-scaling, use Azure Site Recovery for replicating and recovering virtual machines and applications, and leverage Azure Backup and Azure

Storage replication for data backup and recovery.

Q170: What are some best practices for Azure resource management?

Answer: Some best practices for Azure resource management include using resource groups to organize and manage resources, applying tags for easier tracking and billing, implementing role-based access control (RBAC) to manage permissions, using Azure Policy to enforce compliance and governance, and leveraging Azure Resource Manager templates for infrastructure as code.

Q171: What is Azure Logic Apps and how can it be used?

Answer: Azure Logic Apps is a cloud-based service that allows you to automate workflows and integrate different systems and services. It provides a visual designer for creating workflows using pre-built connectors for popular applications and services. Logic Apps can be used to automate business processes, integrate with third-party APIs, and orchestrate complex workflows across different systems.

Q172: How can you monitor and troubleshoot Azure resources and applications?

Answer: Azure provides various monitoring and troubleshooting tools. Azure Monitor allows you to collect and analyze telemetry data from different Azure resources. Azure Application Insights provides application performance monitoring and diagnostics.

Azure Log Analytics enables you to collect, analyze, and visualize log data. Azure Advisor provides recommendations for optimizing resource usage. Azure Service Health provides real-time status and notifications for Azure services. These tools help in monitoring and troubleshooting Azure resources and applications.

Q173: What are Azure Resource Manager templates and how can they be used?

Answer: Azure Resource Manager templates are JSON files that define the infrastructure and configuration of Azure resources. They allow you to deploy and manage resources as a group and enable infrastructure as code practices. Resource Manager templates can be used to create, update, or delete resources in a repeatable and consistent manner. They can be stored in source control and versioned, allowing for easy management and reproducibility of Azure deployments.

Q174: What is Azure Functions Proxies and how can it be used?

Answer: Azure Functions Proxies is a feature of Azure Functions that allows you to create reverse proxies for your functions. It provides a way to expose multiple functions as a single API endpoint and enables URL rewriting, request and response transformations, and caching. Azure Functions Proxies can be used to simplify API management, create composite APIs, and apply custom routing and behavior to your functions.

AZURE INTERVIEW QUESTIONS

Q175: How can you ensure security and compliance in Azure?

Answer: Azure offers several features and services to ensure security and compliance. Azure Security Center provides threat detection and security recommendations. Azure Active Directory enables identity and access management. Azure Key Vault allows you to securely store and manage cryptographic keys and secrets. Azure Policy helps enforce compliance with organizational standards. Additionally, Azure offers various compliance certifications, such as ISO 27001, HIPAA, and GDPR, to meet regulatory requirements.

Q176: What is Azure Data Lake Store and how can it be used?

Answer: Azure Data Lake Store is a scalable and secure data repository for big data analytics workloads. It can store and process large amounts of structured and unstructured data. Azure Data Lake Store provides features like hierarchical file organization, parallel data access, and integration with Azure Data Lake Analytics and other analytics services. It can be used for storing and processing data for data exploration, machine learning, and data analytics.

Q177: What is Azure Service Fabric and when should it be used?

Answer: Azure Service Fabric is a distributed systems platform that simplifies the development, deployment, and management of scalable and reliable microservices-based applications. It provides features like automatic scaling, health monitoring, and service discovery. Azure Service Fabric should be used when building complex, stateful, and highly scalable applications that require fine-grained control over service lifecycle management, reliable communication, and high availability.

Q178: How can you secure data in Azure Storage?

Answer: Azure Storage offers several security features to protect data. You can enable encryption at rest using Azure Storage Service Encryption (SSE) or customer-managed keys (CMK). Azure Storage supports access control through Shared Access Signatures (SAS) and Azure Active Directory (Azure AD) authentication. You can configure network access using Virtual Network Service Endpoints and firewall rules. Azure Storage also provides advanced threat detection and monitoring capabilities through Azure Monitor and Azure Security Center.

Q179: What are the key features of Azure App Service?

Answer: Azure App Service is a fully managed platform for building, deploying, and scaling web, mobile, and API applications. Its key features include automatic scaling to handle traffic fluctuations, built-in support for continuous integration and deployment (CI/CD), integration with Azure DevOps and GitHub, support for multiple programming languages (such as .NET, Java, Node.js), and integration with other Azure services like Azure SQL Database, Azure Functions, and Azure Active Directory.

AZURE INTERVIEW QUESTIONS

Q180: How can you implement high-performance computing (HPC) in Azure?

Answer: Azure provides several services and features for implementing high-performance computing (HPC) workloads. Azure Batch allows you to run parallel and batch computing jobs at scale. Azure CycleCloud provides management and orchestration for HPC clusters. Azure Virtual Machines (VMs) can be configured with high-performance computing capabilities, such as GPUs and InfiniBand networking. Azure HPC Cache can be used for caching data to improve storage performance. Additionally, Azure provides integration with HPC schedulers like Slurm and Grid Engine.

Q181: What is Azure Service Bus and how can it be used?

Answer: Azure Service Bus is a messaging service that enables reliable and scalable communication between applications and services. It supports both pub/sub and point-to-point messaging patterns. Azure Service Bus can be used for decoupling components of distributed systems, implementing event-driven architectures, and ensuring reliable message delivery.

Q182: How can you implement disaster recovery for Azure virtual machines?

Answer: Azure Site Recovery is a service that can be used to implement disaster recovery for Azure virtual machines. It allows you to replicate virtual machines to a secondary Azure region and provides automated failover and failback capabilities. Azure Site

Recovery ensures business continuity by minimizing downtime and data loss in the event of a disaster.

Q183: What is Azure Data Factory and how can it be used?

Answer: Azure Data Factory is a cloud-based data integration service that enables the orchestration and management of data movement and transformation workflows. It supports the extraction, transformation, and loading (ETL) of data from various sources to different destinations. Azure Data Factory can be used to build data pipelines for data integration, data migration, and data transformation scenarios.

Q184: How can you monitor and optimize the performance of Azure SQL Database?

Answer: Azure SQL Database provides built-in performance monitoring and optimization capabilities. You can use features like Query Performance Insight to identify and analyze query performance issues. Dynamic Management Views (DMVs) and Query Store can be used to monitor and troubleshoot query performance. Azure SQL Database also provides automated performance tuning recommendations through Azure Advisor.

Q185: What is Azure IoT Hub and how can it be used?

Answer: Azure IoT Hub is a managed service for connecting, monitoring, and managing Internet of Things (IoT) devices at scale. It provides secure and bidirectional communication between devices and cloud applications. Azure IoT Hub can be used to ingest and process telemetry data from IoT devices, send commands to devices, and implement device management and security features.

Q186: What is Azure Data Factory Data Flow and how can it be used?

Answer: Azure Data Factory Data Flow is a visual data transformation tool within Azure Data Factory. It allows you to build and execute ETL (Extract, Transform, Load) processes for data integration and transformation. Data Flow provides a drag-and-drop interface for designing data transformation logic without writing code, making it easier to build complex data pipelines.

Q187: How can you implement high availability for Azure SQL Database?

Answer: Azure SQL Database provides built-in high availability features. You can configure automatic failover groups to ensure seamless failover to a secondary replica in the event of a planned or unplanned outage. Azure SQL Database also supports geo-replication, allowing you to replicate databases to a secondary region for disaster recovery purposes.

Q188: What is Azure Functions Event Grid and how can it be used?

Answer: Azure Functions Event Grid is an event-based serverless computing platform. It allows you to trigger Azure Functions based on events from various Azure services and custom events. With Event Grid, you can build event-driven architectures and react to events in real-time, enabling seamless integration and automation across different services.

Q189: How can you manage secrets and sensitive data in Azure?
Answer: Azure Key Vault is a service that allows you to securely store and manage secrets, certificates, and keys. You can use Azure Key Vault to centralize and control access to sensitive information, such as database connection strings, API keys, and encryption keys. Azure Key Vault integrates with other Azure services and provides strong security measures, such as encryption at rest and integration with Azure Active Directory for access control.

Q190: What are Azure Logic Apps connectors and how can they be used?
Answer: Azure Logic Apps connectors are pre-built integration connectors that provide connectivity to various external systems and services. Connectors allow Logic Apps to interact with popular applications, such as Salesforce, Office 365, SharePoint, Twitter, and more. They provide a simplified way to integrate workflows and automate business processes by leveraging the capabilities of different systems.

Q191: What is Azure Kubernetes Service (AKS) and how can it be

used?

Answer: Azure Kubernetes Service (AKS) is a managed container orchestration service that simplifies the deployment, management, and scaling of containerized applications using Kubernetes. AKS provides automated scaling, monitoring, and load balancing capabilities. It can be used to deploy and manage containerized applications at scale, leveraging the benefits of Kubernetes for container orchestration.

Q192: How can you implement data backup and restore in Azure?

Answer: Azure provides various services for data backup and restore. Azure Backup allows you to protect and restore data from virtual machines, Azure File shares, SQL databases, and more. Azure Site Recovery enables disaster recovery and replication of virtual machines and physical servers. Azure Blob Storage and Azure Data Lake Storage provide durable and scalable storage for backup data.

Q193: What is Azure Active Directory B2B and how can it be used?

Answer: Azure Active Directory B2B (Business-to-Business) is a feature that allows organizations to collaborate with external users, such as partners and suppliers, while maintaining control over access and security. Azure AD B2B enables organizations to securely share applications, resources, and data with external users, extending their identity and access management capabilities beyond the organization's boundaries.

Q194: How can you implement data encryption in Azure?
Answer: Azure provides several options for data encryption. Azure Storage offers encryption at rest using Azure Storage Service Encryption (SSE) or customer-managed keys (CMK). Azure SQL Database supports transparent data encryption (TDE) to encrypt data at rest. Azure Key Vault can be used to manage encryption keys and secrets. Additionally, Azure Disk Encryption enables encryption of virtual machine disks.

Q195: What is Azure Event Hubs and how can it be used?
Answer: Azure Event Hubs is a scalable event ingestion service that can receive and process millions of events per second. It acts as a central hub for streaming data from various sources, allowing real-time processing and analytics. Azure Event Hubs can be used for scenarios such as log and telemetry ingestion, IoT device telemetry, and real-time analytics on streaming data.

Q196: What is Azure DevOps and how can it be used?
Answer: Azure DevOps is a comprehensive set of development tools and services that facilitate the entire software development lifecycle. It includes features for source code management (Azure Repos), continuous integration and deployment (Azure Pipelines), project tracking and management (Azure Boards), and automated testing (Azure Test Plans). Azure DevOps can be used to plan,

develop, test, and deploy applications efficiently and collaboratively.

Q197: How can you implement serverless computing in Azure?

Answer: Azure provides Azure Functions and Azure Logic Apps for serverless computing. Azure Functions allow you to run small, event-driven code snippets or functions without the need to manage infrastructure. Azure Logic Apps provide a visual designer for building workflows and automating business processes without writing code. Serverless computing in Azure enables cost optimization, automatic scaling, and simplified development and management of applications.

Q198: What is Azure Databricks and how can it be used?

Answer: Azure Databricks is a fast, collaborative Apache Spark-based analytics service. It provides an interactive workspace for data engineers and data scientists to perform data exploration, data preparation, and machine learning tasks. Azure Databricks can be used for big data processing, real-time analytics, and advanced analytics scenarios, leveraging the scalability and performance of Apache Spark.

Q199: How can you implement hybrid connectivity with Azure?

Answer: Azure provides several options for hybrid connectivity. Azure Virtual Network allows you to extend your on-premises network to Azure securely using VPN or ExpressRoute. Azure

Hybrid Connections enable seamless connectivity between Azure and on-premises resources without requiring VPN or network changes. Azure Arc extends Azure management and services to on-premises and multi-cloud environments, providing a consistent control plane for hybrid deployments.

Q200: What are Azure Data Bricks and how can it be used?

Answer: Azure Data Bricks is a fast, easy, and collaborative Apache Spark-based analytics platform. It provides an optimized environment for big data processing, data exploration, and machine learning. Azure Databricks can be used for data engineering tasks, building data pipelines, performing advanced analytics, and developing machine learning models at scale.

Q201: What is Azure Container Instances (ACI) and how can it be used?

Answer: Azure Container Instances (ACI) is a serverless container platform that allows you to run Docker containers without managing the underlying infrastructure. ACI provides on-demand container instances with fast startup times and fine-grained billing. It can be used for running containerized applications, batch jobs, and microservices quickly and efficiently.

Q202: How can you secure Azure resources and applications?

Answer: Azure offers various security measures to protect resources and applications. Some key security features include

Azure Active Directory for identity and access management, Azure Security Center for threat detection and monitoring, Azure Firewall and Network Security Groups for network security, and Azure Key Vault for securely storing and managing secrets and keys. Additionally, you can implement encryption, secure network connections, and follow security best practices to enhance overall security.

Q203: What is Azure Functions Proxies and how can it be used?

Answer: Azure Functions Proxies is a feature of Azure Functions that allows you to create reverse proxies and expose multiple endpoints for your serverless functions. It enables URL rewriting, request/response transformation, and routing rules for your serverless APIs. Azure Functions Proxies can be used to create a facade API layer, aggregate multiple backend services, and provide a unified API interface for client applications.

Q204: How can you implement autoscaling in Azure?

Answer: Azure provides autoscaling capabilities through services like Azure Virtual Machine Scale Sets, Azure App Service, Azure Kubernetes Service (AKS), and Azure Batch. You can configure autoscaling based on metrics such as CPU usage, request queue length, or custom metrics. Autoscaling allows your applications to automatically adjust resources to handle varying workloads, ensuring optimal performance and cost efficiency.

Q205: What is Azure Resource Manager (ARM) and how can it be used?

Answer: Azure Resource Manager (ARM) is a management framework that allows you to deploy, manage, and organize Azure resources as a group. ARM provides a declarative approach to infrastructure provisioning and management using JSON templates. It enables consistent and repeatable deployment of resources, including virtual machines, storage accounts, networking, and more. ARM templates can be used to define the desired state of your infrastructure and manage it as a whole.

Q206: What is Azure Cosmos DB and how can it be used?

Answer: Azure Cosmos DB is a globally distributed, multi-model database service that provides low-latency, scalable, and highly available storage for applications. It supports various data models, including document, key-value, graph, and columnar, allowing flexibility in data modeling. Azure Cosmos DB can be used for building globally distributed applications, real-time analytics, and IoT scenarios that require low-latency access to data.

Q207: How can you monitor and troubleshoot Azure resources and applications?

Answer: Azure provides various monitoring and troubleshooting tools. Azure Monitor allows you to collect and analyze telemetry data from Azure resources, including metrics, logs, and events. Azure Application Insights provides application performance monitoring and diagnostics. Azure Log Analytics enables centralized logging and analysis of log data. Additionally, Azure provides integration with third-party monitoring and observability tools for comprehensive monitoring and troubleshooting.

Q208: What is Azure Managed Kubernetes Service (AKS) and how can it be used?

Answer: Azure Managed Kubernetes Service (AKS) is a fully managed Kubernetes container orchestration service. It simplifies the deployment, management, and scaling of containerized applications using Kubernetes. AKS handles the underlying infrastructure, including provisioning, scaling, and maintenance of the Kubernetes control plane. It can be used to deploy and manage containerized applications with built-in scaling, monitoring, and high availability.

Q209: How can you implement caching in Azure?

Answer: Azure offers various caching options. Azure Cache for Redis provides a fully managed, in-memory caching service that can be used to improve application performance and reduce data access latency. Azure CDN (Content Delivery Network) can be used to cache and deliver static and dynamic content closer to end-users, reducing load on the origin servers. Azure Front Door provides caching and content delivery capabilities at the edge of the Azure network.

Q210: What is Azure Functions Premium Plan and how is it different from the Consumption Plan?

Answer: Azure Functions Premium Plan is an enhanced hosting option for serverless functions. It offers additional features and benefits compared to the Consumption Plan. The Premium Plan provides more consistent and predictable performance, unlimited execution duration, virtual network connectivity, and enhanced scaling controls. It is suitable for scenarios that require advanced features, higher resource allocation, and better isolation for function execution.

Q211: What is Azure Bastion and how can it be used?

Answer: Azure Bastion is a fully managed service that provides secure and seamless RDP and SSH access to Azure virtual machines over the Azure portal. It eliminates the need for public IP addresses or VPN connections to access virtual machines. Azure Bastion enables secure remote access to virtual machines without exposing them to the public internet, enhancing security for remote administration.

Q212: How can you implement disaster recovery for Azure virtual machines?

Answer: Azure Site Recovery is a service that enables disaster recovery of on-premises or Azure virtual machines. It replicates virtual machines to a secondary Azure region and provides automated failover and failback capabilities. By configuring Azure

Site Recovery, you can ensure business continuity and minimize downtime in the event of a disaster or planned maintenance.

Q213: What is Azure ExpressRoute and how can it be used?

Answer: Azure ExpressRoute is a dedicated private connection between on-premises networks and Azure. It provides a high-speed, low-latency, and secure connection, bypassing the public internet. ExpressRoute can be used to extend on-premises networks to Azure, establish hybrid cloud environments, and access Azure services with higher reliability and performance.

Q214: How can you implement identity and access management in Azure?

Answer: Azure Active Directory (Azure AD) is the cloud-based identity and access management service in Azure. It provides capabilities for user management, authentication, and authorization. Azure AD supports single sign-on (SSO) to simplify user access to applications, provides role-based access control (RBAC) for fine-grained access management, and integrates with other Azure services for secure and seamless identity management.

Q215: What is Azure API Management and how can it be used?

Answer: Azure API Management is a fully managed service that helps organizations publish, secure, manage, and analyze APIs. It provides features for API versioning, access control, rate limiting, caching, and analytics. Azure API Management can be used to expose APIs to external partners, developers, and customers securely and efficiently, enabling API monetization and driving API-led digital transformations.

Azure VMs

Q216: What are Azure Virtual Machines (VMs)?

Answer: Azure Virtual Machines (VMs) are scalable computing resources provided by Microsoft Azure. They allow you to create and deploy virtual machines in the cloud, running a variety of operating systems, including Windows and Linux. Azure VMs provide flexibility, scalability, and on-demand provisioning of compute resources.

Q217: What are the different types of Azure VMs?

Answer: Azure VMs come in various types, each optimized for specific workloads. Some common types include General Purpose, Compute Optimized, Memory Optimized, Storage Optimized, GPU, and High-Performance Computing (HPC). The choice of VM type depends on factors such as CPU requirements, memory needs, storage capacity, and specialized workload requirements.

Q218: How can you provision Azure VMs?

Answer: Azure VMs can be provisioned using the Azure portal, Azure CLI (Command-Line Interface), Azure PowerShell, or Azure Resource Manager (ARM) templates. These tools provide different methods for creating, configuring, and managing Azure VMs.

AZURE INTERVIEW QUESTIONS

Q219: How can you secure Azure VMs?

Answer: There are several measures you can take to secure Azure VMs. Some best practices include enabling Azure Security Center for threat detection and monitoring, implementing network security groups and virtual network service endpoints, using Azure Disk Encryption for data protection, applying operating system updates and patches regularly, and enforcing strong authentication and access control.

Q220: How can you scale Azure VMs?

Answer: Azure VMs can be scaled vertically or horizontally. Vertical scaling, also known as scaling up, involves increasing the VM size by adding more CPU cores, memory, or disk space. Horizontal scaling, or scaling out, involves adding more VM instances to distribute the workload. You can use Azure Autoscale to automatically adjust the number of VM instances based on predefined rules.

Q221: How can you backup and restore Azure VMs?

Answer: Azure provides various options for backing up and restoring Azure VMs. Azure Backup can be used to create regular backups of VMs and restore them as needed. Azure Site Recovery enables disaster recovery and replication of VMs to a secondary Azure region. You can also leverage Azure Managed Disks to take point-in-time snapshots for VM disk-level backups.

Q222: How can you monitor Azure VMs?

Answer: Azure provides monitoring capabilities through Azure Monitor. It allows you to collect and analyze metrics, logs, and performance data from Azure VMs. Azure Monitor provides insights into VM health, performance, and availability. You can also set up alerts and notifications based on predefined thresholds to proactively monitor and manage Azure VMs.

Q223: What is Azure VM Scale Sets and how can it be used?

Answer: Azure VM Scale Sets is a feature that allows you to create and manage a group of identical VMs. It provides automatic scaling and load balancing capabilities. VM Scale Sets can be used to build and manage scalable applications, handle increasing workload demands, and ensure high availability by automatically adjusting the number of VM instances based on demand.

Q224: How can you deploy applications to Azure VMs?

Answer: There are multiple ways to deploy applications to Azure VMs. You can use tools like Azure DevOps, Azure CLI, Azure PowerShell, or Azure Resource Manager (ARM) templates to automate application deployments. Additionally, you can leverage containerization technologies like Docker to package applications and deploy them to Azure VMs using container orchestration platforms like Kubernetes or Azure Kubernetes Service (AKS).

AZURE INTERVIEW QUESTIONS

Q225: How can you configure high availability for Azure VMs?

Answer: Azure VMs can be made highly available by using availability sets or availability zones. Availability sets ensure that VM instances are distributed across multiple fault domains and update domains to minimize the impact of planned and unplanned maintenance events. Availability zones provide physically separate locations within an Azure region, allowing VM instances to be spread across multiple zones for enhanced fault tolerance.

Q226: How can you optimize performance for Azure VMs?

Answer: Performance optimization for Azure VMs can be achieved through various techniques. Some approaches include choosing VM sizes that meet the performance requirements of your workload, leveraging premium storage for high IOPS and low latency, optimizing network configurations, using caching mechanisms such as Azure Cache for Redis, and implementing performance tuning strategies at the operating system and application levels.

Q227: How can you automate the management of Azure VMs?

Answer: Azure provides automation capabilities through services like Azure Automation, Azure Virtual Machine Automation, and Azure DevOps. These services allow you to automate VM provisioning, configuration, deployment, and management tasks using scripts, templates, or infrastructure-as-code approaches. Automation helps streamline operations, improve consistency, and reduce manual effort in managing Azure VMs.

Q228: How can you migrate on-premises virtual machines to Azure VMs?

Answer: Azure provides several migration options for moving on-premises VMs to Azure. Azure Migrate is a service that assesses on-premises VMs and provides recommendations for migration. Azure Site Recovery can be used to replicate on-premises VMs to Azure and perform a seamless migration. Additionally, you can use tools like Azure PowerShell or Azure CLI to manually migrate VMs to Azure.

Q229: How can you optimize cost for Azure VMs?

Answer: Cost optimization for Azure VMs can be achieved by right-sizing VM instances based on workload requirements, using Azure Reserved Virtual Machine Instances to save on long-term VM usage, leveraging Azure Hybrid Benefit to apply on-premises Windows Server licenses, scheduling VMs to run only when needed, and using features like Azure Spot VMs or low-priority VMs for non-critical workloads to reduce costs.

Q230: What is Azure Virtual Machine Scale Sets and how does it differ from Azure VMs?

Answer: Azure Virtual Machine Scale Sets allow you to automatically scale a set of VMs based on demand. It's ideal for applications that require consistent scaling, high availability, and load balancing. While Azure VMs are suitable for individual VM deployments, VM Scale Sets are designed for managing and scaling sets of identical VMs as a single unit.

Q231: What is Azure Reserved Virtual Machine Instances and how can it help in cost optimization?

Answer: Azure Reserved Virtual Machine Instances allow you to save costs by pre-paying for Azure VM usage. By committing to a one-year or three-year term, you can enjoy significant savings compared to pay-as-you-go pricing. Reserved Instances provide flexibility by allowing you to exchange or cancel reservations, and they can be applied to VMs in Availability Zones, which further enhances cost savings.

Q232: How can you automate the deployment of Azure VMs using infrastructure-as-code?

Answer: Azure provides various tools for infrastructure-as-code deployments, such as Azure Resource Manager (ARM) templates, Azure Bicep, and Azure CLI. These tools allow you to define the desired state of your infrastructure in a declarative format and automate the provisioning and configuration of Azure VMs. Infrastructure-as-code ensures consistency, repeatability, and version control of your deployments.

Q233: What is Azure Hybrid Benefit, and how does it apply to Azure VMs?

Answer: Azure Hybrid Benefit allows you to apply existing Windows Server licenses with Software Assurance or qualifying SQL Server licenses to reduce the cost of running Azure VMs. By leveraging Azure Hybrid Benefit, you can bring your own licenses and save on VM usage costs. It's a cost-effective option for organizations that already have license agreements with Microsoft.

Q234: How can you ensure high availability for Azure VMs?

Answer: To achieve high availability for Azure VMs, you can use availability sets or availability zones. Availability sets ensure that VM instances are distributed across different fault domains and update domains, minimizing the impact of hardware or software failures. Availability zones provide physically separate data centers within an Azure region, offering redundancy and fault tolerance for your VMs.

Azure Storage Accounts

Q235: What is an Azure Storage Account?

Answer: An Azure Storage Account is a scalable and secure cloud-based storage solution provided by Microsoft Azure. It allows you to store and retrieve various types of data, including blobs, files, tables, and queues. Azure Storage Accounts provide durability, availability, and scalability for storing and accessing data in the cloud.

AZURE INTERVIEW QUESTIONS

Q236: What are the different types of Azure Storage Accounts?

Answer: Azure offers four types of storage accounts: General Purpose v2 (GPv2), General Purpose v1 (GPv1), Blob Storage, and Premium. GPv2 and GPv1 accounts are suitable for a wide range of data types and workloads. Blob Storage accounts are optimized for storing large amounts of unstructured data, such as images or videos. Premium accounts provide high-performance storage for I/O-intensive workloads.

Q237: How can you secure an Azure Storage Account?

Answer: Azure Storage Accounts can be secured using various mechanisms. Some best practices include enabling Azure Storage Service Encryption to encrypt data at rest, configuring shared access signatures (SAS) to control access to storage resources, using Azure Private Link to secure access to storage accounts, and implementing role-based access control (RBAC) to manage permissions and authorization.

Q238: What is the difference between Azure Blob Storage and Azure File Storage?

Answer: Azure Blob Storage is designed for storing unstructured data, such as text files, images, or videos. It provides a simple REST-based interface for accessing and managing blobs. On the other hand, Azure File Storage offers fully managed file shares that can be accessed from multiple VMs simultaneously, providing a distributed file system for applications and virtual machine workloads.

Q239: How can you access data stored in an Azure Storage Account?

Answer: Azure Storage Accounts provide various access methods. The most common methods include using the Azure portal, Azure Storage Explorer, Azure CLI, Azure PowerShell, or Azure SDKs to interact with the storage account programmatically. Additionally, you can access and manage storage account data using REST APIs or Azure Logic Apps for automated workflows.

Q240: How can you replicate data in Azure Storage Accounts for high availability and disaster recovery?

Answer: Azure Storage Accounts offer multiple options for data replication. The available replication options include Locally Redundant Storage (LRS), Zone-Redundant Storage (ZRS), Geo-Redundant Storage (GRS), and Read-Access Geo-Redundant Storage (RA-GRS). These replication options provide various levels of redundancy and data availability across different Azure regions.

Q241: What is the maximum size of an Azure Storage Account?

Answer: The maximum size of an Azure Storage Account depends on the type of account. General Purpose v2 (GPv2) and Blob Storage accounts have a maximum capacity of 5 petabytes (PB). General Purpose v1 (GPv1) accounts have a maximum capacity of 500 terabytes (TB). Premium accounts have a maximum capacity of

100 terabytes (TB).

Q242: How can you enable access control for Azure Storage Accounts?

Answer: Access control for Azure Storage Accounts can be enabled by using Shared Access Signatures (SAS) or Azure Active Directory (Azure AD) authentication. SAS allows you to grant limited permissions and time-limited access to specific storage resources. Azure AD authentication provides more granular control by allowing you to authenticate and authorize users or applications using Azure AD credentials.

Q243: What are the different tiers available for Azure Blob Storage?

Answer: Azure Blob Storage offers three tiers: Hot, Cool, and Archive. The Hot tier is suitable for frequently accessed data with higher storage costs but lower access costs. The Cool tier is designed for infrequently accessed data with lower storage costs but higher access costs. The Archive tier is for long-term retention of rarely accessed data with the lowest storage costs but higher access latency.

Q244: How can you monitor and analyze the usage of Azure Storage Accounts?

Answer: Azure provides various monitoring and analytics features for Azure Storage Accounts. Azure Monitor enables you to collect and analyze metrics and logs for storage account performance and health. Azure Storage Analytics allows you to track storage metrics, analyze logs, and set up retention policies for data. Additionally, you can use Azure Log Analytics and Azure Monitor Logs for advanced analytics and alerting.

Q245: How can you back up and restore data in Azure Storage Accounts?

Answer: Azure Storage Accounts offer built-in backup and restore capabilities. Azure Blob Storage allows you to take snapshots of individual blobs for point-in-time backups. For file shares in Azure File Storage, you can enable Azure File Sync to synchronize file shares with an on-premises file server and leverage traditional backup methods. Additionally, you can use Azure Backup to back up data in Azure VMs that use Azure Storage.

Q246: How can you optimize costs in Azure Storage Accounts?

Answer: To optimize costs in Azure Storage Accounts, you can consider the following strategies: leverage data tiering by storing less frequently accessed data in lower-cost tiers, use lifecycle management to automatically move data to lower-cost tiers or delete it based on defined policies, implement efficient blob storage patterns like block blobs or page blobs depending on the use case, and regularly review and optimize storage account configurations based on actual usage patterns.

AZURE INTERVIEW QUESTIONS

Q247: How can you enable versioning for Azure Blob Storage?

Answer: Versioning in Azure Blob Storage can be enabled at the storage account level. When versioning is enabled, each write operation creates a new version of the blob, allowing you to maintain a complete version history. Versioning helps protect against accidental deletion or modification of data and provides the ability to restore previous versions if needed.

Q248: What is the difference between Azure Blob Storage and Azure Table Storage?

Answer: Azure Blob Storage is designed for storing unstructured data like images, videos, and documents, while Azure Table Storage is a NoSQL key-value store suitable for storing structured data. Blob Storage is ideal for large files or objects, while Table Storage is optimized for storing and querying smaller data elements with low latency.

Q249: How can you secure data in transit for Azure Storage Accounts?

Answer: Data in transit can be secured for Azure Storage Accounts by enabling Transport Layer Security (TLS) encryption for communication. Azure Storage enforces TLS 1.2 as the minimum protocol version. By default, all data sent over public networks, such as accessing storage account endpoints, is encrypted using TLS.

Q250: What is the purpose of the access keys in Azure Storage Accounts?

Answer: Access keys are used for authentication and authorization when accessing Azure Storage Accounts. Each storage account has two access keys: the primary key and the secondary key. These keys provide shared access to the storage account resources and are used to generate Shared Access Signatures (SAS) or authenticate with the storage account from applications or tools.

Q251: How can you replicate data between Azure Storage Accounts in different regions?

Answer: Azure provides options for replicating data between Azure Storage Accounts in different regions. These options include geo-replication using Geo-Redundant Storage (GRS) or Read-Access Geo-Redundant Storage (RA-GRS), which asynchronously replicate data to a secondary region. Additionally, you can use Azure Data Factory or Azure Storage Data Movement Library to perform data replication and synchronization between storage accounts.

Azure Configuration Management

Q252: What is Azure Configuration Management?

Answer: Azure Configuration Management is a service in Azure that helps in managing and tracking the configuration of resources deployed in Azure. It provides a centralized way to define, apply, and track configuration settings for virtual machines, virtual machine scale sets, and Azure virtual machine extensions.

Q253: What are the key benefits of using Azure Configuration Management?

Answer: Some key benefits of using Azure Configuration Management include:

Consistency: Ensuring consistent configuration across multiple resources or environments.

Automation: Enabling automated configuration deployment and management.

Auditing and tracking: Tracking and auditing changes made to configurations.

Compliance: Enabling compliance with regulatory requirements by enforcing configuration standards.

Rapid provisioning: Accelerating the provisioning process by deploying pre-configured resources.

Q254: What are the main components of Azure Configuration Management?

Answer: The main components of Azure Configuration Management are:

Configuration Baseline: It defines the desired configuration for a resource or a set of resources.

Configuration Assignment: It associates a configuration baseline with one or more resources.

Configuration Policy: It defines the compliance requirements for the configuration baseline.

Configuration Remediation: It automatically brings non-compliant resources back into compliance.

Configuration Assessment: It evaluates the compliance of resources against the defined configuration policies.

Q255: How can you apply configurations to Azure resources using Azure Configuration Management?

Answer: Configurations can be applied to Azure resources using the Azure Policy service, Azure Automation State Configuration, or Azure Virtual Machine Extensions. Azure Policy allows you to define and enforce policies that ensure resource configurations meet specific requirements. Azure Automation State Configuration allows you to define and enforce configurations using PowerShell Desired State Configuration (DSC). Azure Virtual Machine Extensions provide a mechanism to install and configure software on virtual machines.

Q256: How does Azure Configuration Management help with compliance and auditing?

Answer: Azure Configuration Management helps with compliance and auditing by providing the ability to define and enforce configuration policies. Configuration policies can be defined to ensure resources adhere to specific configuration standards and compliance requirements. Changes made to resource configurations can be audited and tracked, providing visibility into any configuration drift or non-compliance.

Q257: Can you automate the remediation of non-compliant resources using Azure Configuration Management?

Answer: Yes, Azure Configuration Management enables the automation of remediation for non-compliant resources. When a resource is found to be non-compliant, Azure Configuration Management can automatically apply the necessary configuration changes to bring the resource back into compliance with the defined configuration baseline.

Q258: What is the difference between Azure Policy and Azure Configuration Management?

Answer: Azure Policy focuses on defining and enforcing policies to ensure resource configurations meet specific requirements. It operates at the management plane level and is used to govern resource creation and management. Azure Configuration Management, on the other hand, focuses on applying and tracking configurations for specific resources or sets of resources. It operates at the data plane level and is used to manage the actual configuration settings of resources.

Q259: How can you track and monitor configuration changes in Azure Configuration Management?

Answer: Azure Configuration Management provides built-in tracking and monitoring capabilities. You can use Azure Monitor to track changes made to configuration settings, view audit logs, and set up alerts for configuration drift or non-compliance. Additionally, you can leverage Azure Log Analytics to collect and analyze configuration data, detect anomalies, and gain insights into the configuration state of resources.

Q260: Can you integrate Azure Configuration Management with existing configuration management tools?

Answer: Yes, Azure Configuration Management can integrate with existing configuration management tools. It provides support for PowerShell Desired State Configuration (DSC), allowing you to leverage existing DSC configurations and resources. You can also integrate with popular configuration management tools like Chef and Puppet using Azure Virtual Machine Extensions, which enable you to install and configure these tools on Azure virtual machines.

Q261: What are the deployment options for Azure Configuration Management?

Answer: Azure Configuration Management supports two deployment options:

Azure Portal: You can use the Azure Portal to manually define and apply configurations to individual resources or sets of resources.

Azure Resource Manager (ARM) templates: You can incorporate configuration management into your ARM templates by defining configuration baselines, assignments, and policies. This allows for automated configuration deployment during resource provisioning.

Q262: How does Azure Configuration Management handle configuration drift?

Answer: Azure Configuration Management includes built-in features to detect and remediate configuration drift. Configuration drift occurs when the actual configuration of a resource deviates from the desired configuration. Azure Configuration Management can periodically assess the configuration state of resources, compare it against the desired state defined in the configuration baseline, and automatically remediate any configuration drift by applying the necessary configuration changes.

Q263: How does Azure Configuration Management handle configuration updates?

Answer: Azure Configuration Management allows you to update configurations by modifying the configuration baseline associated with resources. When a configuration baseline is updated, Azure Configuration Management automatically applies the updated configuration to the associated resources. This ensures that resources are always in line with the latest desired configuration.

Q264: Can you provide an example of a use case for Azure Configuration Management?

Answer: One example use case for Azure Configuration Management is maintaining consistent configuration settings across a fleet of virtual machines. By defining a configuration baseline and associating it with a set of virtual machines, you can ensure that all virtual machines have the same configuration settings, such as installed software, security settings, and network configurations.

Q265: How does Azure Configuration Management handle dependencies between configurations?

Answer: Azure Configuration Management allows you to define dependencies between configurations using configuration scripts. Configuration scripts can be written using PowerShell or other scripting languages and can include logic to handle dependencies. For example, if one configuration requires the presence of a specific software package, you can include a script to install that package as part of the configuration.

Q266: Can you automate the deployment of Azure Configuration Management using infrastructure-as-code (IaC)?

Answer: Yes, you can automate the deployment of Azure Configuration Management using infrastructure-as-code (IaC) tools such as Azure Resource Manager (ARM) templates or tools like Terraform. By including the necessary configuration management resources and settings in your IaC templates, you can ensure that Azure Configuration Management is automatically provisioned as part of your infrastructure deployment.

Q267: How can you troubleshoot configuration issues in Azure Configuration Management?

Answer: When troubleshooting configuration issues in Azure Configuration Management, you can leverage the logging and diagnostic capabilities provided by Azure. Azure Monitor and Azure Log Analytics can be used to collect and analyze logs, track changes, and identify any configuration-related errors or inconsistencies. Additionally, you can use PowerShell and Azure CLI commands to retrieve detailed information about configurations and their associated resources.

Azure Automation

Q268: What is Azure Automation?
Answer: Azure Automation is a cloud-based automation service in Azure that allows you to automate the creation, deployment, monitoring, and maintenance of resources in your Azure environment. It provides a way to streamline and automate repetitive tasks, such as provisioning virtual machines, configuring settings, and executing scripts or runbooks.

Q269: What are the key benefits of using Azure Automation?
Answer: Some key benefits of using Azure Automation include:

Increased efficiency: Automating repetitive tasks reduces manual effort and improves efficiency.

Consistency: Ensuring consistent configurations and deployments across multiple resources or environments.

Scalability: Automating resource provisioning and management allows for easy scalability.

Error reduction: Automation reduces the risk of human errors associated with manual tasks.

Time savings: Automated processes save time and enable teams to focus on higher-value activities.

Q270: What are the main components of Azure Automation?

Answer: The main components of Azure Automation are:

Runbooks: Runbooks are automation workflows that contain a series of steps or tasks. They can be authored using PowerShell, Python, or graphical tools.

Assets: Assets are securely stored pieces of data that can be used in runbooks, such as credentials, connection strings, or variables.

Schedules: Schedules define when and how often a runbook should run.

Variables: Variables are used to store and manage values that can be used across runbooks.

Integration modules: Integration modules provide pre-built activities or commands that can be used in runbooks.

Q271: What are the deployment options for Azure Automation?

Answer: Azure Automation provides two deployment options:

Azure Portal: You can use the Azure Portal to manually create, configure, and manage automation resources and runbooks.

Azure Resource Manager (ARM) templates: You can incorporate Azure Automation resources and runbooks into your ARM templates, allowing for automated deployment and management of automation assets.

Q272: How can you trigger the execution of a runbook in Azure Automation?

Answer: Runbooks in Azure Automation can be triggered in several ways:

Schedule: Runbooks can be scheduled to run at specific times or intervals.

Webhook: A webhook can be used to trigger a runbook by making an HTTP request to the webhook URL.

Event-based trigger: Runbooks can be triggered by events from other Azure services, such as the creation of a resource or a change in status.

Q273: How can you securely store and use credentials in Azure Automation?

Answer: Azure Automation provides a feature called "Credentials" where you can securely store and manage usernames and passwords or other secret information. These credentials can be used in runbooks to authenticate with external systems or services without exposing the sensitive information in the script.

Q274: How does Azure Automation integrate with other Azure services?

Answer: Azure Automation integrates with other Azure services through various mechanisms, such as:

PowerShell modules: You can use Azure PowerShell modules within runbooks to interact with and manage Azure resources.

REST APIs: Azure Automation exposes REST APIs that allow you to programmatically interact with automation resources and trigger runbooks.

Webhooks: You can use webhooks to trigger runbooks from external systems or services by making an HTTP request to the webhook URL.

Event Grid: Azure Automation can subscribe to events from Azure Event Grid and trigger runbooks based on specific events or conditions.

Q275: How can you monitor the execution and results of runbooks in Azure Automation?

Answer: Azure Automation provides monitoring and logging capabilities through Azure Monitor. You can enable diagnostics logging for runbooks, view runbook job status and output, and set up alerts for specific conditions, such as failed runbook executions or long-running jobs.

Q276: Can you use source control for managing runbooks in Azure Automation?

Answer: Yes, Azure Automation integrates with source control systems such as Azure DevOps or GitHub. You can store runbook scripts in a source control repository, enable continuous integration and deployment, and automatically update runbooks when changes are made to the repository.

Q277: How can you troubleshoot issues in runbooks in Azure Automation?

Answer: To troubleshoot issues in runbooks in Azure Automation, you can use the following approaches:

Logging and output: Use logging statements and write output to understand the flow and identify any errors or unexpected behavior.

Debug mode: Enable debug mode for runbooks, which allows you to step through the code and inspect variables and objects at runtime.

Exception handling: Implement proper error handling and exception management in runbooks to gracefully handle errors and provide useful error messages.

Diagnostic logs: Enable diagnostics logging for runbooks and review the logs to identify any issues or errors.

Q278: Can you scale Azure Automation to accommodate increased workload demands?

Answer: Yes, Azure Automation can be scaled to accommodate increased workload demands. You can scale Azure Automation by adjusting the number of runbook workers, which are responsible for executing runbooks. By increasing the number of workers, you can handle a higher volume of runbook executions and distribute the workload.

Q279: What is the difference between Azure Automation State Configuration (DSC) and runbooks?

Answer: Azure Automation State Configuration (DSC) is a declarative platform for configuration management that enables you to define and enforce the desired state of resources. It focuses on maintaining the desired configuration state over time. Runbooks, on the other hand, are procedural automation workflows that can execute a series of tasks or actions. While DSC is primarily used for configuration management, runbooks offer broader automation capabilities.

Q280: How can you schedule runbooks in Azure Automation?

Answer: You can schedule runbooks in Azure Automation using the Schedules feature. Within a runbook, you can associate it with a schedule specifying the desired execution time and recurrence pattern. This allows the runbook to be automatically triggered based on the defined schedule.

Q281: Can you pass parameters to runbooks in Azure Automation?

Answer: Yes, runbooks in Azure Automation can accept parameters. Parameters allow you to pass values or arguments to the runbook when it is triggered. This allows for flexibility and customization, as you can dynamically provide input values to the runbook based on specific requirements.

AZURE INTERVIEW QUESTIONS

Q282: How can you enable authentication and authorization for runbooks in Azure Automation?

Answer: Azure Automation supports authentication and authorization through the use of Run As accounts. A Run As account is a service principal that provides the necessary credentials to access and manage Azure resources. By configuring a Run As account and assigning the appropriate permissions, you can ensure that the runbooks in Azure Automation have the necessary credentials and access rights to perform their tasks.

Q283: Can you monitor and track changes to runbooks in Azure Automation?

Answer: Yes, you can monitor and track changes to runbooks in Azure Automation using version control. Azure Automation integrates with source control systems like Azure Repos or GitHub, allowing you to store runbook scripts in a version-controlled repository. This enables you to track changes, view commit history, and easily roll back to previous versions if needed.

Azure Debugging

Q284: What is Azure debugging?

Answer: Azure debugging refers to the process of identifying and resolving issues or errors in Azure applications, services, or resources. It involves investigating and troubleshooting problems to determine the root cause and implement solutions to fix them.

Q285: What are some common tools for debugging Azure applications?

Answer: Some common tools for debugging Azure applications include:

Azure Monitor: Provides monitoring and diagnostics capabilities to collect and analyze telemetry data, logs, and metrics.

Application Insights: A monitoring and application performance management (APM) service that helps track application behavior, performance, and exceptions.

Visual Studio Debugger: A powerful debugging tool provided by Microsoft for debugging Azure applications and services.

Azure Portal Diagnostics: Offers built-in diagnostic tools and logs for Azure resources, such as virtual machines, web apps, and containers.

Q286: How can you debug an Azure Web App?

Answer: To debug an Azure Web App, you can use tools such as Visual Studio or Azure Portal Diagnostics. Here are the general steps:

Enable remote debugging in the Azure Web App settings.

Attach a debugger from Visual Studio to the remote Web App process.

Set breakpoints in your code to pause execution and inspect

variables and application state.

Analyze logs, exceptions, and telemetry data to identify and troubleshoot issues.

Q287: How can you debug an Azure Function?

Answer: To debug an Azure Function, you can use tools such as Visual Studio or the Azure Functions Core Tools. Here are the general steps:

Enable local debugging for Azure Functions in your development environment.

Set breakpoints in your Azure Function code.

Start the debug session in Visual Studio or use the Azure Functions Core Tools to trigger the function locally.

Monitor the execution and inspect variables and function state as the debugger pauses at breakpoints.

Q288: How can you debug an Azure Virtual Machine (VM)?

Answer: To debug an Azure Virtual Machine, you can use remote debugging techniques. Here are the general steps:

Enable remote debugging on the virtual machine.

Configure the necessary firewall rules and network security groups to allow debugging connections.

Connect to the virtual machine using a remote debugging client, such as Visual Studio.

Set breakpoints in your code and analyze the application's behavior, logs, and exceptions while debugging remotely.

Q289: How can you troubleshoot performance issues in Azure applications?

Answer: To troubleshoot performance issues in Azure applications, you can take the following steps:

Monitor and analyze metrics and logs using Azure Monitor or Application Insights.

Identify any performance bottlenecks or high-resource usage patterns.

Optimize code, database queries, or resource configurations to improve performance.

Load test and simulate production-like scenarios to identify and address performance issues before deployment.

Q290: How can you troubleshoot and debug Azure App Service deployment issues?

Answer: To troubleshoot and debug Azure App Service deployment issues, you can:

Check the deployment logs in the Azure portal or using Azure CLI to identify any deployment errors or exceptions.

Enable detailed error messages and remote debugging in the App Service settings.

Use tools like Kudu, which provides a file explorer and diagnostic console for investigating deployment issues.

Review application logs and capture diagnostic data to understand any runtime errors or issues.

Q291: How can you troubleshoot and debug Azure Logic Apps?

Answer: To troubleshoot and debug Azure Logic Apps, you can:

Enable diagnostic logging for your Logic App to capture execution logs and track the flow of actions.

Use the Logic App's built-in run history to view detailed information about each execution and any encountered errors.

Use the Logic App Designer in the Azure portal to inspect and modify the logic flow, inputs, and outputs of individual actions.

Utilize Azure Monitor and Application Insights to monitor and analyze telemetry data, exceptions, and performance metrics.

Q292: How can you diagnose and troubleshoot Azure SQL Database performance issues?

Answer: To diagnose and troubleshoot Azure SQL Database performance issues, you can:

Monitor performance metrics, such as CPU usage, query performance, and resource utilization, using Azure Monitor or Azure SQL Database Insights.

Analyze query plans and execution statistics to identify slow-performing queries and inefficient database operations.

Implement proper indexing and query optimization techniques to improve performance.

Enable Query Store to capture query performance history and identify performance regressions over time.

Q293: How can you troubleshoot and debug Azure Storage issues?

Answer: To troubleshoot and debug Azure Storage issues, you can:

Review the storage account logs and diagnostics data to identify any errors or anomalies.

Use Azure Storage Explorer or Azure portal tools to inspect container, blob, or queue properties and metadata.

Check the access control settings and ensure correct permissions are assigned for accessing storage resources.

Monitor storage metrics, such as throughput, latency, and availability, using Azure Monitor.

Q294: How can you troubleshoot and debug Azure Functions scalability and performance issues?

Answer: To troubleshoot and debug Azure Functions scalability and performance issues, you can:

Monitor execution time and concurrency metrics to identify performance bottlenecks or resource limitations.

Optimize function code for efficiency, including minimizing network calls, optimizing loops, and reducing resource-intensive operations.

Configure scaling settings appropriately based on workload patterns and expected concurrency.

Analyze function logs, exceptions, and telemetry data using Azure Monitor or Application Insights to identify any performance-related issues.

Q295: How can you secure data in Azure Storage?

Answer: You can secure data in Azure Storage using various mechanisms:

Access Control: Use shared access signatures (SAS) to grant limited access to specific resources for a defined period of time.

Encryption: Enable server-side encryption for data at rest using Azure Storage Service Encryption (SSE) or client-side encryption for data in transit.

Virtual Networks: Use virtual network service endpoints and private endpoints to restrict access to Azure Storage from specific networks.

Firewalls and Virtual Networks: Configure network security groups and firewall rules to control inbound and outbound traffic to your storage accounts.

Azure Active Directory: Authenticate access to storage resources using Azure Active Directory (Azure AD) and Azure RBAC for fine-grained access control.

Q296: How can you monitor and optimize the cost of resources in Azure?

Answer: To monitor and optimize the cost of resources in Azure, you can:

Use Azure Cost Management and Billing to track and analyze your resource usage, spending, and trends.

Implement cost allocation tags to categorize resources and gain better visibility into cost distribution.

Utilize Azure Advisor to receive recommendations for optimizing resource utilization and cost.

Implement Azure Automation or Azure Logic Apps to automate cost management tasks, such as starting and stopping resources based on schedules or usage patterns.

Regularly review and optimize resource configurations, such as right-sizing virtual machines or choosing cost-effective storage options.

Q297: How can you ensure high availability for applications in Azure?

Answer: To ensure high availability for applications in Azure, you can:

Use Azure Availability Zones or Azure Regions to deploy resources across multiple data centers to withstand failures in a specific location.

Configure Azure Load Balancer or Azure Application Gateway to distribute incoming traffic across multiple instances of an application.

Implement Azure Traffic Manager for DNS-based traffic routing to different Azure regions or endpoints.

Utilize Azure Virtual Machine Scale Sets or Azure App Service auto-scaling to automatically adjust resources based on demand.

AZURE INTERVIEW QUESTIONS

Implement Azure Site Recovery for disaster recovery and replication of virtual machines or entire applications to a secondary Azure region.

Q298: How can you implement disaster recovery in Azure?

Answer: To implement disaster recovery in Azure, you can:

Use Azure Site Recovery to replicate and failover virtual machines or entire applications to a secondary Azure region.

Utilize Azure Backup to create regular backups of your data and store them in a different Azure region for redundancy.

Implement geo-redundant storage (GRS) or read-access geo-redundant storage (RA-GRS) for Azure Storage accounts to replicate data across multiple regions.

Configure Azure Traffic Manager to automatically redirect traffic to a secondary region in case of a disaster.

Regularly test your disaster recovery plan by performing failover drills and validating the recovery process.

Q299: How can you automate the deployment and management of resources in Azure?

Answer: To automate the deployment and management of resources in Azure, you can:

Use Azure Resource Manager (ARM) templates to define the desired state of your infrastructure as code and deploy resources consistently.

Utilize Azure PowerShell or Azure CLI to script and automate resource provisioning and configuration.

Implement Azure DevOps or Azure Pipelines to set up continuous integration and deployment (CI/CD) pipelines for automated resource deployment.

Use Azure Automation or Azure Logic Apps to orchestrate and automate common management tasks, such as resource start/stop schedules or backups.

Implement infrastructure-as-code tools like Azure Bicep or HashiCorp Terraform for declarative resource provisioning and management.

Azure Networking

Q300: What is Azure Virtual Network (VNet)?

Answer: Azure Virtual Network (VNet) is a fundamental networking service in Azure that allows you to create isolated private networks in the cloud. It provides a secure communication channel between Azure resources, such as virtual machines, and on-premises networks or the internet.

Q301: How can you connect an on-premises network to Azure Virtual Network?

Answer: You can connect an on-premises network to Azure Virtual Network using the following methods:

Site-to-Site VPN: Establish a secure IPsec VPN tunnel between an on-premises VPN device and an Azure VPN Gateway.

ExpressRoute: Create a private connection between your on-premises network and Azure over a dedicated network connection provided by an ExpressRoute partner.

Q302: What is Azure Load Balancer?

Answer: Azure Load Balancer is a traffic distribution service that allows you to balance incoming traffic to multiple backend resources, such as virtual machines or virtual machine scale sets. It improves the availability and scalability of your applications.

Q303: How does Azure Application Gateway differ from Azure Load Balancer?

Answer: While both Azure Application Gateway and Azure Load Balancer are used for load balancing, they have different capabilities:

Azure Application Gateway operates at the application layer (Layer 7) and provides advanced application delivery features, such as SSL termination, URL-based routing, and session affinity.

Azure Load Balancer operates at the transport layer (Layer 4) and provides basic load balancing features, such as distributing traffic based on source IP or port.

Q304: What is Azure Traffic Manager?

Answer: Azure Traffic Manager is a DNS-based traffic routing service that allows you to control the distribution of user traffic to endpoints in different Azure regions or globally. It provides load balancing and failover capabilities to improve application availability and performance.

Q305: What are Network Security Groups (NSGs) in Azure?

Answer: Network Security Groups (NSGs) are Azure resources that act as a basic firewall for controlling inbound and outbound traffic to Azure resources. NSGs allow you to define network security rules to permit or deny specific types of traffic based on source IP, destination IP, port, and protocol.

Q306: How can you secure Azure Virtual Network?

Answer: You can secure Azure Virtual Network using various methods:

Network Security Groups (NSGs): Define inbound and outbound security rules to control traffic flow.

Azure Firewall: Deploy a fully stateful network and application-level firewall to filter traffic in your virtual network.

Azure Private Link: Establish private connectivity between your virtual network and Azure services over the Azure backbone network.

Azure Virtual Network Service Endpoints: Extend your virtual network's private address space to Azure services, keeping traffic within the Azure backbone network.

Azure Virtual Network Peering: Connect virtual networks together to enable cross-network communication using private IP addresses.

AZURE INTERVIEW QUESTIONS

Q307: How can you monitor and troubleshoot Azure networking?

Answer: To monitor and troubleshoot Azure networking, you can use the following tools and services:

Azure Network Watcher: Monitor and diagnose network health, capture packets, and analyze network traffic.

Azure Monitor: Collect and analyze network-related metrics, logs, and diagnostic information.

Azure Log Analytics: Use network-related queries and workbooks to gain insights into network performance and troubleshoot issues.

Azure Network Performance Monitor: Measure and visualize network performance between different endpoints.

Diagnostic Logs and Traffic Analytics: Enable logging and capture traffic data to analyze and troubleshoot network-related issues.

Q308: What is Azure Virtual WAN?

Answer: Azure Virtual WAN is a networking service that provides a unified and optimized connectivity experience for connecting branch offices and remote sites to Azure and other networks. It simplifies network architecture and management by centralizing connectivity and security policies.

Q309: What is Azure ExpressRoute?

Answer: Azure ExpressRoute is a dedicated network connection that provides a private, high-throughput, and low-latency link between your on-premises network and Azure. It offers more reliability, security, and predictable performance compared to internet-based connections.

Q310: What is Azure Firewall and how does it work?

Answer: Azure Firewall is a cloud-native network security service that provides stateful packet inspection and application-level filtering for inbound and outbound traffic in Azure. It operates as a fully stateful firewall as a service, allowing you to control and log traffic at the application and network layers.

Q311: What is Azure DDoS Protection and how does it help in securing applications?

Answer: Azure DDoS Protection is a service that safeguards Azure resources against Distributed Denial of Service (DDoS) attacks. It automatically detects and mitigates DDoS attacks, ensuring the availability and performance of your applications and services.

Q312: What are Azure Network Load Balancer and Azure Application Gateway, and when should you use each?

Answer: Azure Network Load Balancer is a layer 4 load balancing service that distributes incoming traffic at the network level, based on source IP and port. It is ideal for scenarios where you need to balance traffic at the transport layer, such as for TCP and UDP protocols.

Azure Application Gateway, on the other hand, is a layer 7 load balancing service that operates at the application layer and provides advanced application delivery features. It can perform SSL termination, URL-based routing, session affinity, and other application-specific functions.

Use Azure Network Load Balancer when you need simple load balancing at the network layer, and use Azure Application Gateway when you require more advanced application delivery features and routing capabilities.

Q313: How can you secure communication between Azure virtual networks?

Answer: You can secure communication between Azure virtual networks using various methods:

VNet peering: Establish peering connections between virtual networks to allow direct and secure communication using private IP addresses.

Virtual network gateways: Use virtual network gateways to create Site-to-Site VPN or VNet-to-VNet connections to securely connect different virtual networks.

Network Security Groups (NSGs): Apply NSGs to virtual network subnets to control inbound and outbound traffic between virtual networks.

Service endpoints and private endpoints: Use service endpoints and private endpoints to restrict network access to specific Azure services within virtual networks.

Q314: What is Azure ExpressRoute and when would you use it?

Answer: Azure ExpressRoute is a dedicated network connection that provides a private and highly reliable link between your on-premises network and Azure. It is typically used when you require a more predictable network performance, low latency, or need to transfer large amounts of data between your on-premises environment and Azure.

Q315: What is Azure Traffic Manager and how does it work?

Answer: Azure Traffic Manager is a DNS-based traffic routing service that allows you to distribute user traffic across multiple Azure regions or endpoints. It improves application availability and responsiveness by directing users to the nearest or healthiest endpoint based on their location or predefined routing methods.

Q316: What is Azure Active Directory (Azure AD) and how does it relate to Azure?

Answer: Azure Active Directory (Azure AD) is a cloud-based identity and access management service provided by Azure. It serves as the centralized identity provider for Azure services, allowing you to manage user authentication, authorization, and access control. Azure AD is closely integrated with Azure resources and can be used to secure and control access to various Azure services and applications.

AZURE INTERVIEW QUESTIONS

Q317: How can you secure access to Azure resources?

Answer: There are several methods to secure access to Azure resources:

Azure AD authentication: Utilize Azure AD for user authentication and enforce multi-factor authentication (MFA) for added security.

Role-Based Access Control (RBAC): Assign appropriate roles and permissions to users or groups to control access to Azure resources.

Network security: Use network security groups (NSGs), virtual network service endpoints, or private endpoints to restrict inbound and outbound traffic to resources.

Azure Firewall: Deploy Azure Firewall to filter and monitor network traffic to and from Azure resources.

Azure Security Center: Enable Azure Security Center to gain insights into security vulnerabilities, apply security recommendations, and monitor the overall security posture of your Azure resources.

Q318: How can you ensure high availability for applications deployed in Azure?

Answer: To ensure high availability for applications in Azure, you can:

Use Azure Availability Zones or deploy resources across multiple Azure regions to minimize single points of failure.

Utilize Azure Load Balancer or Azure Application Gateway to

distribute incoming traffic and handle failover scenarios.

Implement virtual machine scale sets or Azure App Service auto-scaling to dynamically adjust resources based on demand.

Use Azure Site Recovery to replicate and failover applications to a secondary Azure region for disaster recovery purposes.

Implement monitoring and alerting mechanisms to proactively detect and address potential availability issues.

Q319: How can you monitor the performance and health of Azure resources?

Answer: Azure provides several tools and services for monitoring the performance and health of resources:

Azure Monitor: Collects and analyzes telemetry data from various Azure services and resources, providing insights into performance, availability, and usage.

Azure Application Insights: Helps monitor the performance and availability of applications, providing real-time insights into application health, usage, and user behavior.

Azure Metrics: Captures various performance metrics for Azure resources, such as CPU usage, network throughput, and storage capacity.

Azure Log Analytics: Collects and analyzes log data from Azure resources, allowing you to gain insights, perform troubleshooting, and set up custom monitoring.

Azure Advisor: Provides recommendations to optimize resource performance, security, and cost based on best practices and usage patterns.

Scaling in Azure

Q320: What is scaling in Azure and why is it important?

Answer: Scaling in Azure refers to the ability to dynamically adjust the capacity of your Azure resources based on demand. It is important because it allows you to meet the changing needs of your application or workload, ensuring optimal performance, availability, and cost efficiency.

Q321: What are the different scaling options available in Azure?

Answer: Azure provides several scaling options:

Vertical Scaling: Also known as scaling up, it involves increasing the size (e.g., CPU, memory) of an individual resource, such as a virtual machine.

Horizontal Scaling: Also known as scaling out, it involves adding more instances of a resource, such as virtual machines, to distribute the workload and increase capacity.

Automatic Scaling: Azure provides various services, such as Azure Virtual Machine Scale Sets and Azure App Service, that allow you to configure automatic scaling based on predefined rules or metrics.

Manual Scaling: This involves manually adjusting the capacity of resources as needed.

Q322: What is Azure Virtual Machine Scale Sets?

Answer: Azure Virtual Machine Scale Sets is a service that allows you to create and manage a group of identical virtual machines. It provides automatic scaling capabilities, allowing you to scale out or scale in the number of virtual machines based on demand.

Q323: How does Azure App Service support scaling?

Answer: Azure App Service supports scaling through its App Service Plans. You can select a specific pricing tier for your App Service Plan that determines the capacity and scaling options available. You can scale up by increasing the pricing tier or scale out by adding more instances to the plan.

Q324: How can you configure automatic scaling in Azure?

Answer: Automatic scaling in Azure can be configured using various services, including:

Azure Virtual Machine Scale Sets: You can define scaling rules based on CPU utilization, network traffic, or custom metrics to automatically scale the number of virtual machines in the scale set.

Azure App Service: You can configure auto-scaling rules based on metrics such as CPU, memory, or request count to automatically scale the number of instances.

Azure Functions: You can define scaling rules based on trigger queue length, average execution time, or custom metrics to automatically scale the number of function instances.

Q325: What is Azure Load Balancer and how does it support scaling?

Answer: Azure Load Balancer is a service that distributes incoming network traffic across multiple backend resources, such as virtual machines or virtual machine scale sets. By load balancing the traffic, it improves application availability and allows you to scale out the capacity of your resources.

Q326: How does Azure Autoscale work?

Answer: Azure Autoscale is a feature that allows you to automatically adjust the capacity of your Azure resources based on predefined rules or metrics. It continuously monitors the specified metrics and makes scaling decisions to meet the defined targets. For example, it can scale out resources when CPU utilization exceeds a certain threshold.

Q327: What are some best practices for scaling in Azure?

Answer: Here are some best practices for scaling in Azure:

Use Azure Autoscale or other automatic scaling mechanisms to dynamically adjust resources based on demand.

Monitor key metrics and set appropriate scaling thresholds to ensure resources scale at the right time.

Consider using Azure Virtual Machine Scale Sets or Azure App Service for easy management of scaled resources.

Design your application for horizontal scalability by decoupling components and using distributed architectures.

Regularly test and validate your scaling configuration to ensure it functions as expected under varying workloads.

Q328: What is Azure Application Gateway Autoscaling and how does it work?

Answer: Azure Application Gateway Autoscaling is a feature that automatically adjusts the capacity of an Azure Application Gateway based on the incoming traffic. It uses metrics like CPU utilization, request count, or custom metrics to scale the number of gateway instances up or down, ensuring optimal performance and availability.

Q329: How can you implement auto-scaling for Azure SQL Database?

Answer: Auto-scaling for Azure SQL Database can be implemented using the Azure SQL Database Elastic Pool feature. By creating an elastic pool and adding multiple databases to it, the resource allocation can be dynamically adjusted based on the workload. The elastic pool automatically distributes resources among the databases to handle varying demand.

Q330: What is Azure Container Instances (ACI) and how can you scale it?

Answer: Azure Container Instances (ACI) is a service that allows you to run containerized applications without managing the underlying infrastructure. ACI instances can be scaled by creating multiple container groups or increasing the number of containers within a group. ACI also supports automatic scaling based on CPU or memory utilization.

Q331: What is Azure Kubernetes Service (AKS) and how does it support scaling?

Answer: Azure Kubernetes Service (AKS) is a managed container orchestration service that simplifies the deployment and management of containerized applications using Kubernetes. AKS supports scaling by allowing you to increase or decrease the number of pods (containers) running in a cluster based on workload demands. It provides built-in features like Horizontal Pod Autoscaling (HPA) and Cluster Autoscaler for automatic scaling.

Q332: What are the benefits of using Azure Logic Apps for scaling workflows?

Answer: Azure Logic Apps is a cloud-based service that allows you to create and run workflows for integrating different systems and services. Some benefits of using Azure Logic Apps for scaling workflows include:

Automatic scaling: Logic Apps can automatically scale based on the incoming workload, ensuring that workflows can handle increased demand.

High availability: Logic Apps are highly available, and you can distribute workflows across multiple regions for redundancy and fault tolerance.

Serverless architecture: With serverless execution, you only pay for the resources consumed during workflow execution, allowing for efficient scaling without worrying about infrastructure management.

Q333: What is Azure Functions and how does it support scalability?

Answer: Azure Functions is a serverless compute service that allows you to run code in response to events or triggers. It supports scalability by automatically scaling out and executing function instances based on the incoming workload. This allows your application to handle varying levels of demand without the need to manage infrastructure or provisioning resources.

Q334: How can you scale Azure Blob storage?

Answer: Azure Blob storage can be scaled in two ways:

Vertical Scaling: You can increase the storage capacity of a single blob container by upgrading the storage account to a higher performance tier or increasing the account's storage limit.

Horizontal Scaling: You can distribute the load across multiple blob containers by partitioning data or using techniques like sharding. This allows you to scale out the storage capacity and handle increased workload.

Q335: What is Azure Event Hubs and how does it support

scalability?

Answer: Azure Event Hubs is a highly scalable event streaming platform that can handle millions of events per second. It supports scalability by automatically partitioning event data across multiple partitions. Each partition can be independently scaled, allowing for increased throughput and storage capacity as the workload grows.

Q336: How can you scale Azure SQL Data Warehouse?

Answer: Azure SQL Data Warehouse can be scaled by adjusting the Data Warehouse Units (DWUs). DWUs determine the amount of compute power and resources allocated to the data warehouse. By increasing the number of DWUs, you can scale up the performance and processing capabilities of Azure SQL Data Warehouse.

Q337: What is Azure CDN and how does it support scalability?

Answer: Azure CDN (Content Delivery Network) is a global network of edge servers that caches and delivers content from Azure services and other sources. It supports scalability by caching content closer to end-users, reducing latency and offloading traffic from the origin server. This improves the scalability and performance of applications by distributing content delivery across a globally distributed network.

Monitoring in Azure

Q338: What is Azure Monitor?

Answer: Azure Monitor is a comprehensive monitoring solution in

Azure that provides insights into the performance, availability, and health of your applications and resources. It collects and analyzes telemetry data from various Azure services and allows you to set up alerts, create dashboards, and perform troubleshooting.

Q339: How can you monitor Azure resources using Azure Monitor?

Answer: Azure Monitor provides multiple methods to monitor Azure resources, including:

Metrics: Azure Monitor collects and stores metrics related to various Azure resources, such as virtual machines, databases, and storage accounts. You can view these metrics, set up alerts based on thresholds, and create charts and dashboards.

Logs: Azure Monitor collects logs and events from Azure services, allowing you to analyze and search for specific data. You can query logs using Azure Log Analytics or Azure Monitor Logs and create custom alerts and visualizations.

Application Insights: It is a service within Azure Monitor specifically designed for monitoring application performance. It provides detailed telemetry data, including request rates, response times, and dependency tracking for web applications, APIs, and more.

Q340: What is Azure Diagnostics and how does it work?

Answer: Azure Diagnostics is a feature that allows you to collect and store diagnostic data from Azure resources, such as virtual machines and cloud services. It enables you to capture metrics, logs, and other diagnostic information, which can be used for monitoring, troubleshooting, and performance analysis. The collected data can be sent to Azure Storage, Azure Event Hubs, or Azure Log Analytics for further analysis.

Q341: How can you set up alerts in Azure Monitor?

Answer: You can set up alerts in Azure Monitor using the following steps:

Define the condition: Specify the metric or log query that triggers the alert when it meets certain criteria, such as CPU usage exceeding a threshold or specific log events occurring.

Set the action: Define the action to be taken when the alert is triggered, such as sending an email notification, triggering an Azure Function, or scaling out resources.

Configure the alert rule: Specify the scope of the alert, which resources it applies to, and the frequency of evaluation.

Test and enable the alert: Validate the alert configuration and enable it to start monitoring and triggering notifications based on the defined conditions.

Q342: What is Azure Service Health?

Answer: Azure Service Health is a feature of Azure Monitor that provides information about the health and availability of Azure services in the regions where you have resources deployed. It gives you insights into ongoing issues, planned maintenance events, and health advisories related to Azure services, helping you stay informed about any potential impact on your resources.

Q343: How can you monitor and analyze log data in Azure Monitor?

Answer: You can monitor and analyze log data in Azure Monitor using Azure Log Analytics. Log Analytics provides a powerful query language and visualization capabilities to search, analyze, and correlate log data from various sources. You can create custom queries, build dashboards, set up alerts, and even perform advanced analytics using machine learning and AI capabilities.

Q344: What is Azure Application Insights and how does it help in monitoring applications?

Answer: Azure Application Insights is a service within Azure Monitor that helps monitor the performance and availability of applications. It provides detailed telemetry data, including request rates, response times, and dependency tracking. With Application Insights, you can identify and diagnose application issues, track user interactions, analyze application performance trends, and set up alerts for specific metrics or exceptions.

Q345: How can you monitor Azure virtual machines (VMs) using Azure Monitor?

Answer: Azure Monitor provides insights into Azure VMs through metrics, diagnostics logs, and Azure Monitor for VMs. You can monitor metrics such as CPU usage, memory utilization, and network traffic. Diagnostics logs can capture events, system logs, and performance counters. Azure Monitor for VMs offers enhanced monitoring capabilities, including VM performance views, insights into the host OS, and integration with Azure Security Center.

Q346: What are Log Analytics workspaces in Azure Monitor?

Answer: Log Analytics workspaces are centralized repositories for log data in Azure Monitor. They provide a consolidated location to collect, analyze, and correlate logs from various sources, including Azure resources and on-premises environments. Log Analytics workspaces enable efficient log data management, querying, visualization, and alerting capabilities across multiple sources and services.

Q347: How can you set up diagnostic settings for Azure resources?

Answer: Diagnostic settings in Azure allow you to configure how diagnostic data is collected and sent to Azure Monitor. You can enable diagnostic settings for specific Azure resources, such as virtual machines or Azure App Service. By specifying the desired diagnostic data types, destination, and retention period, you can ensure that the relevant logs, metrics, or events are captured and made available for monitoring and analysis.

Q348: What is Azure Advisor, and how does it help in monitoring

and optimization?

Answer: Azure Advisor is a free service that provides recommendations to optimize Azure resources for performance, high availability, security, and cost efficiency. It analyzes resource configurations, usage patterns, and best practices to provide actionable insights. Azure Advisor recommendations help in monitoring and optimizing your Azure environment to ensure optimal performance, resource utilization, and cost savings.

Q349: What is Azure Log Analytics and how does it work?

Answer: Azure Log Analytics is a service that allows you to collect, analyze, and query log and performance data from various sources. It provides a central repository for log data, enabling you to perform advanced analytics, create custom queries, and build visualizations and dashboards. Log Analytics uses the Log Analytics workspace as the container for log data, and you can collect data from Azure resources, on-premises environments, and third-party sources.

Q350: How can you create custom dashboards in Azure Monitor?

Answer: Azure Monitor provides the ability to create custom dashboards to visualize and monitor your Azure resources and applications. You can use the Azure portal or Azure Dashboard JSON templates to design and configure dashboards. By selecting the relevant metrics, logs, and visual elements, you can create personalized dashboards that provide real-time insights into the health, performance, and usage of your resources.

Q351: What are action groups in Azure Monitor and how are they used?

Answer: Action groups in Azure Monitor are a way to define a list of actions to be taken when an alert is triggered. They allow you to specify the notifications and actions that need to be performed, such as sending email notifications, SMS messages, webhook calls, or triggering Azure Functions or Logic Apps. Action groups provide flexibility and extensibility in defining how you want to be notified and what automated actions should be taken when an alert is raised.

Q352: How can you use Azure Monitor to track and analyze application performance?

Answer: Azure Monitor provides Application Insights, which is specifically designed for monitoring application performance. Application Insights allows you to track various performance metrics, such as request rates, response times, and failure rates. It also provides dependency tracking, allowing you to identify performance bottlenecks and troubleshoot issues. Application Insights integrates with Azure Monitor, providing a comprehensive solution for monitoring and analyzing application performance.

Q353: How can you monitor and analyze security-related events in Azure?

Answer: Azure Monitor provides Azure Security Center integration to monitor and analyze security-related events. It enables you to collect security-related data, including security alerts, vulnerability assessments, and threat intelligence. You can use Azure Monitor to query and analyze this data, detect security threats, and gain insights into the security posture of your Azure environment.

Azure High Avilability

Q354: What is high availability in Azure?

Answer: High availability refers to the ability of a system or application to remain operational and accessible even in the event of failures or disruptions. In Azure, high availability is achieved by implementing redundant and fault-tolerant architectures, such as deploying resources across availability zones or using features like Azure Load Balancer and Azure Traffic Manager.

Q355: What are availability zones in Azure and how do they contribute to high availability?

Answer: Availability zones are physically separate data centers within an Azure region. Each availability zone has its own power, cooling, and networking infrastructure. By deploying resources across availability zones, you can ensure that your applications and services remain available even if one zone experiences a failure. Availability zones provide built-in redundancy and fault tolerance.

AZURE INTERVIEW QUESTIONS

Q356: How can you design a highly available architecture in Azure?

Answer: To design a highly available architecture in Azure, you can consider the following:

Use availability sets or availability zones to distribute resources across fault domains and update domains.

Implement load balancing using Azure Load Balancer or Azure Application Gateway to distribute traffic across multiple instances or availability zones.

Use Azure Traffic Manager for global load balancing and failover across regions.

Implement automated scaling to handle fluctuations in demand and ensure sufficient capacity.

Use Azure Backup and Azure Site Recovery for data protection and disaster recovery.

Q357: What is the purpose of Azure Traffic Manager?

Answer: Azure Traffic Manager is a DNS-based traffic load balancer that enables high availability and automatic failover across different regions or endpoints. It allows you to distribute incoming traffic based on various traffic-routing methods, such as performance, priority, or geographic proximity. Azure Traffic Manager helps in achieving high availability by directing users to the most optimal and available endpoint.

Q358: How can you achieve high availability for virtual machines

in Azure?

Answer: To achieve high availability for virtual machines in Azure, you can:

Use availability sets or availability zones to distribute VMs across fault domains and update domains.
Configure VM auto-scaling to automatically adjust the number of VM instances based on demand.
Use Azure Load Balancer to distribute incoming traffic across multiple VMs.
Configure Azure VM Scale Sets to provide automatic scaling and fault tolerance for a group of VMs.

Q359: What is the purpose of Azure Load Balancer?

Answer: Azure Load Balancer is a traffic distribution service that helps in achieving high availability and scalability for applications. It distributes incoming traffic across multiple backend resources, such as virtual machines or virtual machine scale sets, to ensure that the workload is evenly distributed and the application remains accessible even if some resources become unavailable.

Q360: What is Azure Availability Zones and how do they differ from Azure Availability Sets?

Answer: Azure Availability Zones are physically separate data centers within an Azure region, offering redundant power, cooling, and networking. They provide a higher level of fault tolerance compared to Azure Availability Sets, which distribute virtual machines across fault domains and update domains within a single data center. Availability Zones provide resiliency at the infrastructure level, while Availability Sets provide resiliency at the virtual machine level.

Q361: How can you ensure high availability for Azure Storage accounts?

Answer: To ensure high availability for Azure Storage accounts, you can enable geo-redundant storage (GRS) or zone-redundant storage (ZRS). GRS replicates data synchronously across multiple regions, providing automatic failover in case of a region-wide failure. ZRS replicates data synchronously across multiple zones within a region, providing redundancy against zone-level failures. Both options help maintain data availability and durability.

Q362: What is Azure Traffic Manager's failover routing method?

Answer: Azure Traffic Manager offers several routing methods, including the failover routing method. With failover routing, you can configure a primary endpoint and one or more secondary endpoints. If the primary endpoint becomes unavailable, Traffic Manager automatically directs traffic to one of the secondary endpoints. This helps ensure high availability by enabling automatic failover in case of endpoint failures.

Q363: How does Azure Load Balancer handle inbound and outbound traffic?

Answer: Azure Load Balancer can handle both inbound and outbound traffic. For inbound traffic, it distributes incoming requests across multiple backend resources, such as virtual machines or virtual machine scale sets, to achieve high availability and load balancing. For outbound traffic, Azure Load Balancer uses source network address translation (SNAT) to provide outbound connectivity for virtual machines, allowing them to communicate with the internet or other resources.

Q364: How can you achieve high availability for Azure SQL Database?

Answer: To achieve high availability for Azure SQL Database, you can enable the "Business Critical" or "Premium" service tier, which provides built-in high availability through active geo-replication. Active geo-replication asynchronously replicates the database to a secondary region, allowing for automatic failover in case of a primary region failure. This ensures minimal downtime and data loss for your SQL Database.

Q365: What is Azure Resource Manager (ARM), and what is its role in Azure?

Answer: Azure Resource Manager (ARM) is the deployment and management service in Azure. It provides a consistent and unified way to deploy, manage, and organize Azure resources. ARM templates are used to define the desired state of Azure resources and their relationships, allowing for repeatable and automated deployments. ARM simplifies resource management by providing a single API endpoint and a set of tools for managing Azure resources.

Q366: What are Azure Virtual Networks, and what are their key features?

Answer: Azure Virtual Networks enable you to create isolated and secure networks in Azure. They allow you to define IP address ranges, subnets, and network security groups to control network traffic. Virtual Networks can be connected to on-premises networks or other Azure Virtual Networks through VPN or Azure ExpressRoute. Key features of Azure Virtual Networks include virtual network peering, network security groups, and Azure DNS integration.

Q367: How can you secure Azure resources and data?

Answer: To secure Azure resources and data, you can implement various security measures, including:

Implementing role-based access control (RBAC) to grant appropriate permissions to users and groups.
Using Azure Active Directory for user authentication and single sign-on.
Enabling Azure Security Center to monitor and detect security threats.
Encrypting data at rest and in transit using Azure Storage Service

Encryption and Azure SSL/TLS certificates.

Implementing network security groups and firewall rules to control inbound and outbound traffic.

Q368: What is Azure App Service, and what are its key features?

Answer: Azure App Service is a fully managed platform for building, deploying, and scaling web and mobile applications. It supports multiple programming languages and frameworks, including .NET, Java, Node.js, and Python. Key features of Azure App Service include automatic scaling, continuous deployment from various source control systems, integration with Azure Active Directory for authentication and authorization, and support for custom domains and SSL certificates.

Q369: What is Azure Functions, and how can they be used?

Answer: Azure Functions is a serverless computing service in Azure. It allows you to run event-driven functions without worrying about infrastructure management. Functions can be triggered by various events, such as HTTP requests, timers, or messages from Azure Event Grid or Azure Service Bus. Azure Functions are useful for building serverless applications, implementing microservices architectures, and automating tasks.

Storage in Azure

Q370: What are the different types of storage services available in Azure?

Answer: Azure offers several storage services, including:

Azure Blob storage: Used to store unstructured data like images, documents, and videos.

Azure File storage: Provides fully managed file shares accessible via the SMB protocol.

Azure Table storage: A NoSQL key-value store for semi-structured data.

Azure Queue storage: A messaging service for asynchronous communication between components of an application.

Azure Disk storage: Provides managed virtual hard disks for VMs.

Q371: What is the difference between Azure Block Blob and Page Blob?

Answer: Azure Block Blob is optimized for storing large amounts of unstructured data and supports streaming scenarios. It is ideal for scenarios like media storage and backups. On the other hand, Azure Page Blob is designed for random read/write operations and is commonly used for storing virtual machine disks.

Q372: How can you secure data in Azure Storage?

Answer: You can secure data in Azure Storage by implementing the following measures:

Use Azure RBAC to control access to storage accounts.

Enable Azure Storage service encryption to encrypt data at rest.

Configure Shared Access Signatures (SAS) to grant limited access to specific resources.

Use Azure Private Link to secure access to storage accounts over a private network connection.

Implement firewall and virtual network rules to control inbound and outbound traffic.

Q373: How does Azure Blob storage handle data durability?

Answer: Azure Blob storage automatically replicates data to provide durability and high availability. By default, Blob storage creates three copies of the data within the storage account. The replicas are stored in different fault domains and upgrade domains to ensure redundancy and protect against hardware failures.

Q374: What is the purpose of Azure Storage Explorer?

Answer: Azure Storage Explorer is a tool that allows you to manage and interact with Azure storage resources. It provides a graphical user interface for viewing and managing storage accounts, uploading and downloading files, creating and deleting containers, and managing shared access signatures. It simplifies the management of Azure storage resources for developers and administrators.

Q375: How can you enable versioning for Azure Blob storage?

Answer: Versioning is not natively supported in Azure Blob storage. However, you can implement versioning by using a combination of techniques, such as appending a version number to the blob name, leveraging blob metadata, or using Azure Blob storage lifecycle management to archive older versions of blobs.

AZURE INTERVIEW QUESTIONS

Q376: What is Azure Files and how does it differ from Azure Blob storage?

Answer: Azure Files is a fully managed file share service in Azure, accessible via the SMB protocol. It allows you to create file shares that can be accessed by multiple virtual machines or applications. Unlike Azure Blob storage, which is optimized for unstructured data storage, Azure Files provides shared file storage, similar to traditional file servers, making it suitable for scenarios that require shared file access across multiple VMs or applications.

Q377: How can you monitor Azure Storage performance and availability?

Answer: Azure provides several monitoring options for Azure Storage, including:

Azure Monitor: Allows you to set up alerts and monitor metrics such as request latency, successful and failed requests, and storage capacity.

Storage Analytics: Enables you to collect and analyze detailed storage metrics, including ingress and egress traffic, transactions, and storage capacity.

Azure Log Analytics: Offers powerful log search and analysis capabilities for Azure Storage logs, allowing you to identify issues and troubleshoot performance problems.

Q378: What is Azure Data Lake Storage and how is it different

from Azure Blob storage?

Answer: Azure Data Lake Storage is a scalable and secure data lake solution in Azure. It is optimized for big data analytics and can store structured, semi-structured, and unstructured data. Azure Data Lake Storage provides a hierarchical namespace that enables efficient data organization and supports parallel processing. Unlike Azure Blob storage, which is more suitable for general-purpose storage, Azure Data Lake Storage is designed specifically for big data workloads.

Q379: What is the purpose of Azure Queue storage?

Answer: Azure Queue storage is a messaging service in Azure that allows you to decouple components of an application by providing asynchronous communication. It is commonly used for building scalable and loosely coupled systems. Applications can write messages to queues, and other applications or components can read and process those messages independently. Azure Queue storage provides reliable message delivery and helps to improve application responsiveness and scalability.

Q380: How does Azure Storage support high availability and disaster recovery?

Answer: Azure Storage provides built-in replication options for high availability and disaster recovery. These include:

Locally redundant storage (LRS): Replicates data within a single data center for high availability.

Zone-redundant storage (ZRS): Replicates data across multiple availability zones within a region, providing higher durability and availability.

Geo-redundant storage (GRS): Replicates data to a secondary region, providing additional protection against regional outages.

Q381: What is the purpose of Azure Storage Account Keys, and how are they used?

Answer: Azure Storage Account Keys are used for authentication and authorization to access the resources within a storage account. They act as the primary credentials for accessing the storage account and its associated services, such as Blob storage, Table storage, and Queue storage. Storage Account Keys should be kept secure and not shared openly. They can be used in API calls or through client libraries to authenticate and gain access to the storage account.

Q382: What is the difference between Azure Premium Storage and Standard Storage?

Answer: Azure Premium Storage is designed for high-performance workloads that require low latency and high IOPS (Input/Output Operations Per Second). It uses solid-state drives (SSDs) for storage, providing faster disk performance compared to Standard Storage. On the other hand, Azure Standard Storage uses magnetic drives (HDDs) and is suitable for most general-purpose storage needs with moderate performance requirements.

Q383: How does Azure Blob storage handle data redundancy and durability?

Answer: Azure Blob storage provides redundancy and durability by automatically replicating data within the storage account. It offers three types of redundancy:

Locally redundant storage (LRS): Data is replicated within a single storage scale unit in a data center, providing high availability within that location.

Zone-redundant storage (ZRS): Data is replicated across multiple availability zones within a region, ensuring higher availability and durability.

Geo-redundant storage (GRS): Data is replicated to a secondary region, providing additional protection against regional failures or disasters.

Q384: What is the purpose of Azure Storage Explorer, and how can it be used?

Answer: Azure Storage Explorer is a graphical user interface (GUI) tool that allows you to manage Azure storage accounts easily. It provides a convenient way to browse and manage Blob storage containers, queues, tables, and file shares. With Storage Explorer, you can upload and download files, create and delete containers, manage shared access signatures (SAS), and view storage account properties. It is a valuable tool for developers and administrators working with Azure storage resources.

Q385: How can you optimize costs when using Azure Blob storage?

Answer: To optimize costs in Azure Blob storage, consider the following strategies:

Use Azure Blob storage lifecycle management to automatically move data to lower-cost tiers (e.g., from hot to cool storage, or cool to archive storage) based on predefined rules.

Leverage blob-level tiering to manually manage the storage tier based on access patterns.

Use block blobs for storing large amounts of unstructured data, as they offer cost-effective storage options.

Consider using Azure Blob storage static website hosting for hosting static web content, which can be more cost-efficient than deploying and managing a separate web server.

Q386: What is the difference between Azure Blob storage and Azure File storage?

Answer: Azure Blob storage is designed for storing unstructured data, such as documents, images, and videos, in a scalable and cost-effective manner. On the other hand, Azure File storage provides fully managed file shares that can be accessed via the standard SMB (Server Message Block) protocol. Azure File storage is suitable for scenarios where shared file access is required, such as lift-and-shift applications or shared file storage across multiple VMs.

Q387: What is Azure Storage Service Encryption (SSE) and how does it work?

Answer: Azure Storage Service Encryption (SSE) is a feature that automatically encrypts data at rest in Azure storage accounts. SSE encrypts the data before storing it and decrypts it when accessed. It uses Microsoft-managed keys to provide transparent encryption and decryption of data without any additional configuration or code changes required from the user. SSE is available for all Azure storage services and helps ensure the confidentiality and security of data stored in Azure.

Q388: How can you enable access control for Azure Storage resources?

Answer: Azure provides several access control mechanisms for Azure Storage resources:

Azure RBAC (Role-Based Access Control): You can assign roles to users, groups, or applications to control their permissions on storage accounts and resources.

Shared Access Signatures (SAS): SAS allows you to grant time-limited access to specific resources within a storage account, with granular permissions such as read, write, or delete.

Azure AD (Azure Active Directory) authentication: You can configure Azure Storage to authenticate access using Azure AD credentials, providing more centralized and fine-grained access control.

Q389: What is Azure Blob storage lifecycle management, and how can it be used?

Answer: Azure Blob storage lifecycle management allows you to define policies to automatically transition blobs between different access tiers (hot, cool, and archive) based on specific criteria. It helps optimize costs by automatically moving data to the most appropriate storage tier as it ages or based on custom-defined rules. For example, you can configure a policy to move data to the cool tier after 30 days of inactivity and then to the archive tier after 90 days of inactivity, thereby reducing storage costs for infrequently accessed data.

Q390: How can you monitor and diagnose performance issues in Azure Storage?

Answer: Azure provides several monitoring and diagnostics capabilities for Azure Storage, including:

Azure Monitor: You can configure metrics and alerts to monitor storage account performance, such as ingress/egress rates, transaction rates, and latency.

Storage Analytics: It enables you to collect and analyze detailed metrics and logs for Azure Storage, including transaction logs, capacity metrics, and availability data.

Azure Storage Insights: It provides visualizations and insights into storage account performance, helping identify performance bottlenecks and troubleshoot issues.

Azure AD

Q391: What is Azure Active Directory (Azure AD)?

Answer: Azure Active Directory (Azure AD) is a cloud-based identity and access management service provided by Microsoft. It serves as a central hub for managing user identities, authentication, and authorization in Azure and other Microsoft services. Azure AD enables secure and seamless sign-on experiences, multi-factor authentication, role-based access control, and integration with various applications and services.

Q392: What are the different editions of Azure AD?

Answer: Azure AD offers different editions to cater to different organizational needs:

Azure AD Free: This edition provides basic identity and access management capabilities, including user and group management, single sign-on (SSO), and self-service password reset.

Azure AD Basic: In addition to the features in the Free edition, Azure AD Basic includes enterprise-level SSO, group-based access management, and self-service password reset for cloud users.

Azure AD Premium P1: This edition includes advanced features such as self-service group management, advanced security reports and alerts, Azure AD Application Proxy, and dynamic group membership.

Azure AD Premium P2: This edition offers all the features of P1, along with additional capabilities like Azure AD Identity Protection, Privileged Identity Management, and Azure AD Conditional Access.

Q393: What is Azure AD B2C, and how does it differ from Azure AD?

Answer: Azure AD B2C (Business-to-Consumer) is a service within Azure AD that enables organizations to provide secure and customizable identity management for their customer-facing applications. It is designed for applications that require customer registration, login, and profile management. Azure AD B2C allows you to create branded and user-friendly sign-in experiences, support social identity providers, and customize user flows. In contrast, Azure AD focuses on managing employee and organizational identities for business-to-business (B2B) and business-to-employee (B2E) scenarios.

Q394: How can you enforce multi-factor authentication (MFA) in Azure AD?

Answer: Azure AD provides several methods to enforce multi-factor authentication (MFA) for user sign-in:

Conditional Access: You can create policies in Azure AD Conditional Access to require MFA based on specific conditions, such as user location, device type, or application sensitivity.

Azure AD Identity Protection: It offers risk-based policies that can automatically trigger MFA if suspicious or risky sign-in activities are detected.

Azure AD Security Defaults: This is a pre-configured set of security policies that enforces MFA for all users in an Azure AD tenant.

Q395: How can you integrate on-premises Active Directory with Azure AD?

Answer: Azure AD provides several options for integrating on-premises Active Directory with Azure AD:

Azure AD Connect: It is a tool that synchronizes user accounts, passwords, and groups between on-premises AD and Azure AD. This enables users to have a single identity across both environments and allows for seamless authentication and access to Azure resources.

Azure AD Federation: You can configure federation between on-premises AD and Azure AD using protocols such as Security Assertion Markup Language (SAML) or OpenID Connect. This allows users to authenticate against the on-premises AD infrastructure while accessing Azure services.

Q396: What is Azure AD Application Proxy, and how does it work?

Answer: Azure AD Application Proxy is a feature that enables remote access to on-premises web applications through Azure AD. It allows users to securely access internal applications from anywhere, without the need for a VPN. Azure AD Application Proxy works by creating an outbound connection from the on-premises environment to the Azure AD Application Proxy service. Requests from external users are routed through Azure AD, which then securely forwards the requests to the on-premises application.

Q397: What is Azure AD B2B collaboration, and how does it work?

Answer: Azure AD B2B collaboration enables organizations to securely collaborate with users from other organizations. It allows external users to access resources in the organization's Azure AD tenant without requiring them to have a separate user account. Azure AD B2B collaboration works by inviting external users to collaborate on specific resources or applications. The external users can authenticate using their own organization's credentials or a Microsoft account, and they can be assigned roles and permissions to access the shared resources.

Q398: What is Azure AD Domain Services, and what is its purpose?

Answer: Azure AD Domain Services is a managed domain service that provides compatibility with traditional on-premises Active Directory. It allows you to join Azure virtual machines to a domain, use Group Policy for managing domain-joined machines, and authenticate users with their domain credentials. Azure AD Domain Services eliminates the need for running domain controllers on-premises and enables cloud-only or hybrid scenarios where you need to leverage Active Directory features without managing the infrastructure.

Q399: What is Azure AD Privileged Identity Management (PIM)?

Answer: Azure AD Privileged Identity Management is a service that helps manage, control, and monitor access to privileged roles in Azure AD and other Azure resources. It allows organizations to reduce the exposure of privileged accounts by providing just-in-time access and enforcing strong access controls. Azure AD PIM enables role assignments to be time-bound, requires approval for activation, and provides auditing capabilities to track and monitor privileged access.

Q400: How can you monitor and audit Azure AD activities?

Answer: Azure AD provides several monitoring and auditing capabilities to track and analyze user activities:

Azure AD Sign-ins: You can monitor and analyze user sign-in activities, including successful and failed sign-in attempts, from the Azure AD Sign-ins report.

Azure AD Audit logs: These logs provide detailed information about changes and events within Azure AD, such as user and group management, role assignments, and application registrations.

Azure AD Identity Protection: It offers risk-based policies and detection mechanisms to identify and respond to potential identity threats or vulnerabilities.

Q401: What is Azure AD Connect, and what is its role in Azure AD integration?

Answer: Azure AD Connect is a tool used to synchronize on-premises Active Directory identities and attributes with Azure AD. It enables organizations to have a unified identity across on-premises and cloud environments. Azure AD Connect synchronizes user accounts, passwords, and group memberships, allowing users to have a single identity and enabling seamless access to resources in both environments.

Q402: What is Azure AD Conditional Access, and how does it work?

Answer: Azure AD Conditional Access is a policy-based access control feature that allows you to enforce specific conditions for granting access to Azure AD-connected applications and resources. It enables organizations to define policies based on factors like user location, device compliance, application sensitivity, and risk levels. Azure AD Conditional Access helps protect resources by ensuring that users meet specific criteria before accessing sensitive data or applications.

Q403: What are the authentication methods supported by Azure AD?

Answer: Azure AD supports various authentication methods,

including:

Password-based authentication: Users authenticate using a username and password.

Multi-Factor Authentication (MFA): Users are required to provide additional verification, such as a one-time password or biometric authentication, in addition to their password.

Azure AD Smart Lockout: It detects and mitigates brute-force attacks by locking out an account temporarily after a specified number of unsuccessful sign-in attempts.

Azure AD Identity Protection: It provides adaptive authentication and risk-based policies to detect and respond to potential identity threats.

Q404: What is Azure AD Application Insights, and how can it be used?

Answer: Azure AD Application Insights is a feature that provides detailed telemetry and monitoring capabilities for Azure AD-integrated applications. It helps developers track application performance, usage patterns, and user behaviors. Azure AD Application Insights collects data on authentication events, token validations, and user interactions, allowing developers to gain insights into application usage, identify performance bottlenecks, and troubleshoot issues.

Q405: How can you enable self-service password reset for Azure AD users?

Answer: Azure AD provides self-service password reset (SSPR) capabilities for users to reset their passwords without administrative assistance. SSPR can be enabled and configured in the Azure AD portal, allowing users to verify their identity through methods like email, phone, or security questions. By enabling SSPR, organizations can reduce the burden on helpdesk teams and enhance user productivity.

Azure Service bus mapping

Q406: What is Azure Service Bus mapping?
Answer: Azure Service Bus mapping is a feature that allows you to define rules for message routing within an Azure Service Bus topic or subscription. With mapping, you can define filter conditions based on message properties and create rules that determine which messages get forwarded to specific subscriptions. This enables you to route and filter messages based on various criteria, such as message content, custom properties, or system properties.

Q407: How do you define mapping rules in Azure Service Bus?
Answer: Mapping rules in Azure Service Bus are defined using SQL-like filter expressions. These expressions evaluate message properties and determine the routing of messages. You can specify conditions based on message properties, including user-defined properties and system properties like MessageId, Label, and CorrelationId. By defining mapping rules, you can direct messages

to specific subscriptions based on the defined criteria.

Q408: What are the benefits of using mapping in Azure Service Bus?

Answer: The benefits of using mapping in Azure Service Bus include:

Dynamic message routing: Mapping allows you to dynamically route messages to different subscriptions based on their properties, enabling flexible and targeted message delivery.

Message filtering: You can define filter conditions in mapping rules to filter out unwanted messages, ensuring that only relevant messages are delivered to the desired subscriptions.

Scalability and performance: By using mapping, you can distribute the message workload across multiple subscriptions, which can improve scalability and performance in scenarios where there is a high volume of messages.

Simplified message handling: Mapping helps simplify message handling by automatically routing messages based on their properties, reducing the need for manual intervention or additional logic in the consuming applications.

Q409: Can you have multiple mapping rules for a single subscription in Azure Service Bus?

Answer: Yes, you can have multiple mapping rules for a single subscription in Azure Service Bus. Each mapping rule specifies a condition and an action. When a message arrives, the mapping engine evaluates the conditions of each rule sequentially until a match is found. If multiple mapping rules match the message, the rule with the highest numeric value for the SequenceNumber property takes precedence.

Q410: How can you update mapping rules in Azure Service Bus?

Answer: To update mapping rules in Azure Service Bus, you need to modify the filter expressions associated with the rules. This can be done programmatically using the Service Bus SDKs or through the Azure portal. When updating mapping rules, it's important to consider the potential impact on message routing and ensure that the changes align with the desired message handling and distribution requirements.

Q411: What is Azure Key Vault, and what is its purpose?

Answer: Azure Key Vault is a cloud-based service that allows you to securely store and manage cryptographic keys, secrets, and certificates. Its purpose is to provide a centralized and secure location for storing sensitive information that is used to authenticate, encrypt, or sign data in Azure applications. Azure Key Vault helps protect keys and secrets from unauthorized access and provides a secure way to manage and use cryptographic assets within your applications.

Q412: What are the different deployment models in Azure, and what are their characteristics?

Answer: Azure supports two main deployment models: the Azure Service Manager (ASM) model, also known as the classic deployment model, and the Azure Resource Manager (ARM) model, the newer and recommended model. The ASM model focuses on individual resources and has limitations in terms of scalability and management. In contrast, the ARM model provides a more holistic and template-based approach to deploy and manage resources, offering enhanced scalability, security, and management capabilities.

Q413: What is Azure Virtual WAN, and how does it simplify networking?

Answer: Azure Virtual WAN is a networking service that simplifies and optimizes connectivity for branch offices to Azure and other branch offices. It provides a unified hub-and-spoke architecture, allowing you to connect and manage multiple branches using a central hub. Azure Virtual WAN simplifies networking by automating the deployment and configuration of virtual network gateways, VPN connections, and routing policies. It helps streamline branch connectivity, improves performance, and enhances network security.

Q414: How does Azure Active Directory (Azure AD) differ from on-premises Active Directory?

Answer: Azure AD is a cloud-based identity and access management service, whereas on-premises Active Directory (AD) is a traditional directory service used for managing identities within an organization's network. While both provide similar capabilities like user authentication and authorization, Azure AD extends these functionalities to cloud resources and applications, allowing for seamless single sign-on, federation, and integration with various SaaS applications. Azure AD also offers additional features such as conditional access, multi-factor authentication, and self-service password reset.

Q415: What is Azure Functions, and how can it be used?

Answer: Azure Functions is a serverless compute service in Azure that allows you to run code in response to events or triggers without the need to manage infrastructure. It enables you to execute code in a serverless manner, paying only for the actual execution time. Azure Functions can be used for various purposes, such as building event-driven applications, creating serverless APIs, automating tasks through scheduled functions, and integrating with other Azure services to build serverless workflows.

Q416: What is Azure Logic Apps, and how does it work?

Answer: Azure Logic Apps is a cloud-based service that provides a way to automate business processes and workflows by orchestrating tasks, data, and services across different systems. Logic Apps uses a visual designer where you can define a series of steps and connectors to integrate with various services and trigger actions based on events. It supports a wide range of connectors, allowing you to create powerful workflows that can automate tasks, integrate systems, and streamline business processes.

Q417: What is Azure App Service, and what are its key features?

Answer: Azure App Service is a fully managed platform for building, deploying, and scaling web and mobile applications. It provides a rich set of features, including automatic scaling, continuous deployment, high availability, and integration with Azure services. App Service supports multiple programming languages and frameworks, making it flexible for application development. It also offers built-in features like authentication, monitoring, and diagnostics to help developers streamline the application lifecycle.

Q418: What is Azure DevOps, and how can it be used?

Answer: Azure DevOps is a set of development tools and services that facilitate collaboration, automation, and continuous integration and delivery (CI/CD) in software development projects. It provides features for source code management, build automation, testing, and release management. Azure DevOps enables teams to plan, develop, test, and deliver software efficiently and reliably. It offers integrations with popular development tools, allowing teams to build and deploy applications with ease.

Q419: What is Azure Data Factory, and how does it support data integration and orchestration?

Answer: Azure Data Factory is a cloud-based data integration service that enables you to create, schedule, and orchestrate workflows for data movement and data transformation across various data sources and destinations. It provides a visual interface for building data pipelines, allowing you to define data ingestion, transformation, and movement activities. Azure Data Factory supports hybrid scenarios, allowing you to connect to on-premises data sources and cloud-based services, making it a powerful tool for data integration and orchestration.

Q420: What is Azure Load Balancer, and how does it work?
Answer: Azure Load Balancer is a traffic distribution service that distributes incoming network traffic across multiple resources or virtual machines within a virtual network. It helps improve availability and scalability of applications by evenly distributing traffic and automatically routing around failed resources. Azure Load Balancer supports both inbound and outbound scenarios and can be configured for various protocols and load-balancing algorithms. It plays a critical role in building highly available and scalable applications in Azure.

Azure Key vaults

Q421: What is Azure Key Vault, and what is its purpose?
Answer: Azure Key Vault is a cloud service that allows you to securely store and manage cryptographic keys, secrets, and

certificates. Its purpose is to provide a centralized and secure location for storing sensitive information that is used to authenticate, encrypt, or sign data in Azure applications. Azure Key Vault helps protect keys and secrets from unauthorized access and provides a secure way to manage and use cryptographic assets within your applications.

Q422: How can you access and manage secrets in Azure Key Vault?

Answer: Secrets in Azure Key Vault can be accessed and managed programmatically using the Azure Key Vault REST API or through SDKs for various programming languages, such as .NET, Java, Python, and PowerShell. These APIs and SDKs allow you to perform operations like creating secrets, retrieving secrets, updating secrets, and deleting secrets. Additionally, Azure Key Vault provides RBAC (Role-Based Access Control) to control access to secrets and supports integration with Azure services for seamless secret retrieval and management.

Q423: How does Azure Key Vault protect secrets?

Answer: Azure Key Vault employs several security measures to protect secrets, including encryption at rest and in transit, access policies, RBAC, and audit logging. Secrets stored in Azure Key Vault are encrypted using industry-standard algorithms, and Azure Key Vault supports Hardware Security Modules (HSMs) for enhanced security. Access to secrets can be restricted using fine-grained access policies and RBAC, ensuring that only authorized users and applications can access them. Additionally, Azure Key Vault logs all access and usage information, enabling audit and compliance requirements.

Q424: Can you store other types of sensitive data besides secrets in Azure Key Vault?

Answer: Yes, besides secrets, Azure Key Vault can also be used to store and manage other types of sensitive data, including cryptographic keys and certificates. Azure Key Vault supports various key types, such as RSA keys, EC keys, and symmetric keys, which can be used for encryption, signing, and decryption operations. Additionally, Azure Key Vault can store and manage X.509 certificates, allowing you to securely manage certificates used for SSL/TLS communication, code signing, and other purposes.

Q425: How can you monitor and audit Azure Key Vault activities?

Answer: Azure Key Vault provides extensive monitoring and auditing capabilities. You can enable diagnostic logging for Azure Key Vault to capture detailed information about operations, errors, and other events. This log data can be sent to Azure Monitor or Azure Storage for analysis and monitoring. Additionally, Azure Key Vault integrates with Azure Monitor, allowing you to set up alerts and notifications based on specific conditions or events. These monitoring and auditing features help you track and analyze activities in Azure Key Vault for security, compliance, and troubleshooting purposes.

Q426: How can you authenticate and authorize access to Azure Key Vault?

Answer: Azure Key Vault supports various authentication mechanisms, including Azure Active Directory (Azure AD), managed identities for Azure resources, and shared access signatures (SAS). Azure AD integration allows you to authenticate users and applications using Azure AD credentials and apply fine-grained access control through RBAC. Managed identities provide a secure way for Azure resources to authenticate and access Key Vault without the need for explicit credentials. Shared access signatures enable you to generate time-limited access tokens with specific permissions for accessing Key Vault resources.

Q427: Can you provide an example of how to retrieve a secret from Azure Key Vault programmatically?

Answer: Certainly! Here's an example using the Azure SDK for .NET and the C# programming language:

```csharp
Copy code
using Azure.Identity;
using Azure.Security.KeyVault.Secrets;

var keyVaultName = "<YourKeyVaultName>";
```

```csharp
var secretName = "<YourSecretName>";

var client = new SecretClient(new Uri($"https://{keyVaultName}.vault.azure.net"), new DefaultAzureCredential());

KeyVaultSecret secret = await client.GetSecretAsync(secretName);

string secretValue = secret.Value;
Console.WriteLine($"Retrieved secret value: {secretValue}");
```

This example demonstrates how to use the Azure SDK and the SecretClient class to retrieve a secret from Azure Key Vault. It utilizes the DefaultAzureCredential for authentication, which automatically uses the available credentials in the environment (Azure AD, managed identity, or Visual Studio credentials).

Q428: What is soft delete in Azure Key Vault, and how does it work?

Answer: Soft delete is a feature in Azure Key Vault that allows you to recover deleted keys, secrets, and certificates within a retention period. When soft delete is enabled, deleted items are moved to a recovery state, preventing immediate permanent deletion. During the retention period, you can restore the deleted items or permanently delete them. Soft delete provides an added layer of data protection and allows you to recover accidentally deleted keys or secrets.

Q429: How does Azure Key Vault integrate with Azure Virtual Machines (VMs)?

Answer: Azure Key Vault integrates with Azure VMs by leveraging Azure Managed Service Identity (MSI). MSI provides a secure way for VMs to obtain tokens without the need for explicit credentials. By enabling MSI on the VM and granting the necessary permissions in Azure Key Vault, you can allow the VM to authenticate with Key Vault and access secrets or keys directly without exposing sensitive information in the VM configuration.

Q430: How can you enable and manage access policies in Azure Key Vault?

Answer: Access policies in Azure Key Vault control permissions for managing and accessing resources. You can configure access policies to grant permissions to users, groups, or applications. To manage access policies, you can use the Azure portal, Azure PowerShell, Azure CLI, or Azure SDKs. Access policies allow you to define permissions for operations such as getting and setting secrets, managing keys, and managing certificates. By assigning appropriate access policies, you can control and restrict access to Azure Key Vault resources.

Q431: What is Azure Virtual Network (VNet), and what are its key features?

Answer: Azure Virtual Network (VNet) is a fundamental building block in Azure networking, allowing you to create isolated and secure networks in the cloud. Key features of Azure VNet include:

Network isolation: VNets provide network isolation and segmentation, allowing you to control traffic flow and secure communication between resources.

Subnetting: VNets can be divided into multiple subnets to further segregate resources based on their security or functional requirements.

Connectivity options: VNets offer connectivity options such as VNet-to-VNet peering, site-to-site VPN, and ExpressRoute to establish connections with on-premises networks or other Azure VNets.

Network security: VNets support network security groups (NSGs) and Azure Firewall to enforce network-level security policies and control inbound and outbound traffic.

Private IP address space: You can define your own private IP address ranges within a VNet to avoid IP conflicts with other networks.

Q432: What is Azure Load Balancer, and how does it work?

Answer: Azure Load Balancer is a traffic distribution service that allows you to distribute incoming network traffic across multiple resources or virtual machines within a virtual network. Key points about Azure Load Balancer include:

Load balancing algorithms: Azure Load Balancer supports various load-balancing algorithms, including round-robin, source IP affinity, and least connections, to evenly distribute traffic across resources.

Health probes: Load Balancer continuously monitors the health of backend resources using health probes and automatically routes traffic only to healthy resources.

Inbound and outbound scenarios: Azure Load Balancer can be used for both inbound and outbound scenarios. Inbound Load Balancer distributes incoming traffic to resources, while outbound Load Balancer provides a single egress point for traffic leaving a VNet.

Public and internal Load Balancer: Azure Load Balancer can have a public IP address assigned to it to handle public-facing traffic or an internal IP address for internal load balancing within a VNet.

Highly available and scalable: Azure Load Balancer is highly available and can scale to handle high traffic loads. It automatically scales up or down based on demand.

Q433: What is Azure Functions, and how does it work?

Answer: Azure Functions is a serverless compute service that allows you to run event-driven code without managing infrastructure. Key points about Azure Functions include:

Event-driven execution: Azure Functions can be triggered by various events, such as HTTP requests, timers, message queues, storage events, and more.

Supported languages: Azure Functions supports multiple programming languages, including C#, JavaScript, Python,

PowerShell, and TypeScript.

Pay-per-use pricing: Azure Functions follows a consumption-based pricing model, where you only pay for the execution time of your functions and the resources used.

Scalability: Azure Functions automatically scales to accommodate incoming requests. It can handle high traffic and scale down to zero when there is no workload, reducing costs.

Integration with other Azure services: Azure Functions seamlessly integrates with other Azure services, such as Azure Storage, Azure Event Grid, Azure Service Bus, and more, enabling you to build powerful serverless workflows.

Q434: What is Azure Container Instances (ACI), and how does it differ from Azure Kubernetes Service (AKS)?

Answer: Azure Container Instances (ACI) is a serverless containerization service that allows you to run Docker containers without managing the underlying infrastructure. Key points about ACI include:

Easy container deployment: ACI provides a simple and quick way to deploy containers without the need to manage VMs or orchestration frameworks.

Granular billing: With ACI, you are billed based on the resources consumed by your containers, such as CPU, memory, and storage, providing granular cost control.

Single container focus: ACI is designed for running single containers or task-based workloads, making it ideal for small-scale deployments or burst scenarios.

Azure Kubernetes Service (AKS), on the other hand, is a managed container orchestration service that simplifies the deployment, management, and scaling of containerized applications using Kubernetes.

AKS provides advanced features like automatic scaling, self-healing, service discovery, and rolling updates, making it suitable for larger, complex, and production-grade containerized applications.

Q435: What is Azure Site Recovery, and how does it help with disaster recovery?

Answer: Azure Site Recovery is a disaster recovery service that helps protect and recover your applications and workloads in the event of a datacenter outage. Key points about Azure Site Recovery include:

Replication and failover: Azure Site Recovery replicates virtual machines and physical servers from a primary site to a secondary site, providing continuous data protection.

Site recovery orchestration: It automates the orchestration of failover and failback processes, ensuring minimal downtime and data loss during disaster recovery scenarios.

Cross-platform support: Azure Site Recovery supports replication and failover for both on-premises and Azure-based workloads, including VMware, Hyper-V, and physical servers.

Application-aware recovery: It provides application-level

consistency during recovery by integrating with applications like SQL Server, Exchange, SharePoint, and more.

Testing and non-disruptive recovery: Azure Site Recovery allows you to perform planned or unplanned failover testing without impacting the production environment, ensuring confidence in your disaster recovery plans.

Azure web and mobile Services

Q436: What is Azure App Service, and what are its key features?

Answer: Azure App Service is a fully managed platform for building, deploying, and scaling web and mobile applications. Key features of Azure App Service include:

Multiple runtime support: Azure App Service supports various programming languages, frameworks, and platforms such as .NET, Java, Node.js, Python, PHP, and Ruby.

Scalability and autoscaling: It allows you to scale your application horizontally by increasing the number of instances or vertically by upgrading the instance size. Autoscaling can be configured based on metrics like CPU utilization or request count.

Continuous deployment: Azure App Service integrates with popular source control systems like Azure DevOps, GitHub, and Bitbucket, enabling continuous integration and deployment of applications.

High availability and fault tolerance: It provides built-in load balancing, automatic OS and runtime patching, and built-in disaster recovery capabilities to ensure high availability and fault tolerance.

Integration with Azure services: Azure App Service seamlessly integrates with other Azure services such as Azure SQL Database, Azure Storage, Azure Functions, and Azure Active Directory, enabling easy development and integration of applications.

Q437: What is Azure Logic Apps, and how does it work?

Answer: Azure Logic Apps is a cloud-based service that allows you to create workflows and integrate various applications, systems, and services. Key points about Azure Logic Apps include:

Workflow design: Logic Apps provide a visual designer to create workflows using a drag-and-drop interface, making it easy to define the sequence of actions and triggers.

Pre-built connectors: It offers a wide range of connectors for popular applications and services, including Azure services, Office 365, Salesforce, Twitter, Dropbox, and more.

Trigger-based execution: Logic Apps can be triggered by events such as HTTP requests, timers, incoming messages, or changes in data sources, enabling event-driven workflows.

Data transformation and manipulation: It provides a rich set of actions for data transformation, manipulation, and conditional branching within the workflow.

Scalability and monitoring: Azure Logic Apps can automatically scale based on the load and provide monitoring and tracking capabilities to analyze the execution of workflows.

Q438: What is Azure SignalR Service, and how does it help in

AZURE INTERVIEW QUESTIONS

real-time communication?

Answer: Azure SignalR Service is a fully managed service that simplifies the integration of real-time communication capabilities into web and mobile applications. Key points about Azure SignalR Service include:

Real-time messaging: SignalR Service enables real-time bi-directional communication between clients and server applications, allowing instant updates and notifications.

Scalability and performance: It automatically scales the backend infrastructure to handle high traffic and concurrent connections, ensuring low latency and high performance.

Protocol abstraction: SignalR supports multiple real-time communication protocols, including WebSockets, Server-Sent Events, and Long Polling, providing seamless connectivity across different clients.

Cross-platform support: It offers SDKs for various platforms and programming languages, such as .NET, JavaScript, Java, Python, and more, enabling easy integration with different client applications.

Integration with Azure services: SignalR Service integrates with other Azure services, such as Azure Functions, Azure App Service, and Azure Logic Apps, allowing you to build real-time applications with ease.

Q439: What are Azure Mobile Apps (formerly known as Azure Mobile Services)?

Answer: Azure Mobile Apps is a set of services and tools provided by Azure for building mobile backends. Key points about Azure Mobile Apps include:

Backend as a Service (BaaS): Azure Mobile Apps provides backend functionalities such as user authentication, data storage, push notifications, offline data sync, and social integration, allowing developers to focus on building mobile app frontends.

Cross-platform support: It offers SDKs and client libraries for various mobile platforms, including iOS, Android, Windows, Xamarin, and Cordova, facilitating app development across different devices.

Integration with Azure services: Azure Mobile Apps seamlessly integrates with other Azure services like Azure SQL Database, Azure Storage, Azure Functions, and Azure Notification Hubs, enabling comprehensive backend functionalities.

Easy scalability and monitoring: Mobile Apps can scale automatically based on the demand, and Azure provides monitoring and diagnostics tools for tracking app usage, performance, and error reporting.

Offline synchronization: Azure Mobile Apps provides offline data synchronization capabilities, allowing mobile apps to work seamlessly even when there is no network connectivity.

Q440: What is Azure Functions, and how does it differ from

AZURE INTERVIEW QUESTIONS

Azure App Service?

Answer: Azure Functions is a serverless compute service that allows you to run code in a serverless manner. It executes code in response to events and can be used to build small, single-purpose functions. Here's how Azure Functions differs from Azure App Service:

Execution model: Azure App Service runs web applications continuously, while Azure Functions runs code only when triggered by events. Functions are event-driven and executed on demand.

Scalability: Azure App Service can be scaled manually or automatically based on the instance count or size. Azure Functions scales automatically and dynamically based on the incoming workload and demand.

Billing: Azure App Service is billed based on the runtime and instance usage. Azure Functions is billed based on the number of executions and the execution duration.

Code structure: Azure App Service allows you to build full-fledged web applications with multiple endpoints and business logic. Azure Functions focuses on small, modular functions that perform a specific task or respond to a specific event.

Integration: Both Azure App Service and Azure Functions can integrate with other Azure services, but Azure Functions has deeper integrations with event-driven services like Azure Event Grid and Azure Service Bus.

Q441: What is Azure Mobile Engagement, and how does it help in user engagement?

Answer: Azure Mobile Engagement (now deprecated and replaced by Visual Studio App Center) was a service that enabled mobile app developers to analyze and engage users. Key points about Azure Mobile Engagement include:

User analytics: Azure Mobile Engagement provided detailed user analytics, such as app usage, session duration, user demographics, and custom events, helping developers understand user behavior.

Push notifications: It allowed developers to send personalized push notifications to specific user segments based on their behavior or predefined criteria, increasing user engagement and retention.

In-app feedback: Azure Mobile Engagement offered a feedback mechanism within the app, enabling users to provide feedback and report issues directly from the app interface.

A/B testing: It facilitated A/B testing by allowing developers to create multiple versions of app content and measure user engagement and conversion rates for each variant.

Campaign management: Azure Mobile Engagement provided tools for creating and managing marketing campaigns, including personalized messages, targeted offers, and in-app promotions.

Note: As mentioned earlier, Azure Mobile Engagement has been deprecated, and its functionality has been integrated into Visual Studio App Center, which offers a broader range of services for mobile app development and engagement.

AZURE INTERVIEW QUESTIONS

Q442: What is Azure CDN (Content Delivery Network), and how does it improve website performance?

Answer: Azure CDN is a global distributed network of servers that caches and delivers content from websites and other internet-based services. Here's how Azure CDN improves website performance:

Reduced latency: Azure CDN caches static content, such as images, CSS, and JavaScript files, on servers located closer to the end-users. This reduces the round-trip time and improves the website's response time.

Bandwidth optimization: By offloading static content delivery to Azure CDN, the origin server's bandwidth usage is reduced, allowing it to focus on handling dynamic requests more efficiently.

Scalability: Azure CDN automatically scales to handle high traffic and concurrent requests, ensuring consistent performance even during peak usage periods.

Global reach: Azure CDN has a widespread presence across multiple geographic regions, enabling content to be delivered from the server closest to the end-user, minimizing network latency.

DDoS protection: Azure CDN provides DDoS (Distributed Denial of Service) protection, mitigating potential attacks and ensuring the availability of content.

Q443: What is Azure Notification Hubs, and how does it facilitate push notifications?

Answer: Azure Notification Hubs is a scalable, cross-platform push notification service. Here's how it facilitates push notifications:

Cross-platform support: Azure Notification Hubs supports sending push notifications to various platforms, including iOS, Android, Windows, and Xamarin, allowing developers to reach a wide range of devices.

Registration and targeting: Notification Hubs handles device registration and management, enabling targeted notifications based on user segments, tags, or specific device criteria.

Scale and performance: It can handle millions of notifications simultaneously, ensuring high performance and delivery reliability even during peak loads.

Templated notifications: Notification Hubs supports templated notifications, where developers can define notification templates with placeholders for dynamic content, making it easier to send personalized notifications.

Integration with backend systems: Azure Notification Hubs integrates with other Azure services like Azure Functions, Azure Logic Apps, and Azure Mobile Apps, allowing seamless integration with backend systems for triggering push notifications based on specific events or conditions.

Q444: What is Azure Mobile Authenticator, and how does it enhance app security?

Answer: Azure Mobile Authenticator is a feature of Azure Active Directory that provides two-factor authentication for mobile apps. Here's how it enhances app security:

Two-factor authentication: Azure Mobile Authenticator adds an extra layer of security by requiring users to provide a second form of verification, typically through a mobile app, in addition to their username and password.

Mobile app verification: Users can install the Azure Authenticator app on their mobile devices, which generates time-based one-time passwords (TOTPs) or push notifications for authentication.

Multi-factor authentication policies: Azure Active Directory allows administrators to define policies that enforce two-factor authentication for specific users, groups, or applications, enhancing security for sensitive resources.

Conditional Access: Azure Active Directory's Conditional Access policies can be used to require two-factor authentication based on factors such as user location, device health, or the sensitivity of the accessed resource.

Seamless user experience: Azure Mobile Authenticator offers a user-friendly and intuitive experience for two-factor authentication, making it easy for users to verify their identities without disrupting their app usage.

Azure Projects

Q445: What is an Azure Resource Manager (ARM) template, and how does it help in managing Azure projects?

Answer: Azure Resource Manager (ARM) templates are JSON files that define the infrastructure and configuration of Azure resources.

Here's how they help in managing Azure projects:

Answer: Azure DevOps is a set of development tools and services provided by Microsoft for software development and project management. It offers a range of features, including source control, continuous integration/continuous deployment (CI/CD), project tracking, and collaboration tools. Here are a few key points about Azure DevOps:

Source control: Azure DevOps provides version control systems like Git, allowing teams to manage and track changes to their codebase.

CI/CD pipelines: It enables the creation of automated build and release pipelines, allowing for continuous integration and deployment of applications.

Work item tracking: Azure DevOps offers work item tracking features, including backlog management, sprint planning, and issue tracking, providing a centralized platform for project management.

Testing and artifact management: It supports various testing frameworks and provides artifact management capabilities for storing and sharing build artifacts.

Collaboration and reporting: Azure DevOps provides features for team collaboration, including dashboards, code reviews, and team notifications. It also offers reporting and analytics to track project progress and identify areas for improvement.

Q446: How does Azure DevOps integrate with Azure services?

Answer: Azure DevOps integrates seamlessly with various Azure services, allowing for streamlined application development and deployment. Here are a few examples of Azure service integrations:

Azure Repos: Azure DevOps integrates with Azure Repos, a version control service, enabling teams to manage their code repositories directly within the Azure DevOps platform.

Azure Pipelines: Azure DevOps provides built-in support for Azure Pipelines, allowing teams to create CI/CD pipelines for building, testing, and deploying applications to Azure services.

Azure Boards: Azure Boards, the project management and tracking feature of Azure DevOps, can be used to track work items and issues related to Azure resources and deployments.

Azure Artifacts: Azure Artifacts, the artifact management service, integrates with Azure DevOps to store and manage build artifacts and package dependencies for easy sharing and consumption.

Azure Monitor: Azure DevOps integrates with Azure Monitor to provide insights into application performance and health, allowing teams to monitor and troubleshoot their deployed applications.

Q447: What is Azure DevTest Labs, and how can it benefit Azure projects?

Answer: Azure DevTest Labs is a service that allows developers and IT professionals to quickly provision and manage development and testing environments in Azure. Here's how it can benefit Azure projects:

Rapid environment provisioning: Azure DevTest Labs enables the quick creation of pre-configured environments, including virtual machines, containers, and other resources, reducing the setup time for development and testing.

Cost optimization: It provides cost management features like auto-shutdown and virtual machine size restrictions, helping to optimize resource usage and reduce costs associated with development and testing environments.

Resource management: Azure DevTest Labs allows administrators to define policies for resource usage, access, and quotas, ensuring efficient resource utilization and maintaining control over environments.

Integration with CI/CD pipelines: It integrates seamlessly with Azure Pipelines, enabling developers to easily incorporate DevTest Labs into their CI/CD pipelines for automated environment provisioning and testing.

Self-service environment creation: Developers can self-service provision their required environments from pre-defined templates, reducing the dependency on IT operations for environment setup.

Q448: What is Azure Resource Manager (ARM), and how does it facilitate infrastructure deployment and management?

Answer: Azure Resource Manager (ARM) is the deployment and management service for Azure resources. Here's how it facilitates infrastructure deployment and management:

AZURE INTERVIEW QUESTIONS

Template-based deployment: ARM uses JSON-based templates to define and deploy infrastructure resources consistently and repeatedly, allowing for infrastructure as code and enabling version-controlled deployments.

Resource grouping: ARM allows resources to be grouped logically into resource groups, simplifying management, deployment, and monitoring of related resources.

Dependency management: ARM handles dependencies between resources, automatically deploying dependent resources before their dependents, ensuring proper resource provisioning and configuration.

Role-based access control: ARM integrates with Azure Active Directory and provides role-based access control (RBAC), allowing fine-grained control over resource access and management permissions.

Deployment and management operations: ARM provides APIs and command-line tools for deploying, updating, and managing Azure resources, enabling automation and integration with other tools and processes.

Q449: How does Azure Resource Manager (ARM) support infrastructure scalability and high availability?

Answer: ARM provides features and capabilities that support infrastructure scalability and high availability in Azure projects:

Scale sets: ARM allows the creation of virtual machine scale sets, which automatically scale based on demand, ensuring that the application can handle increased traffic and workload.

Load balancing: ARM supports load balancers, allowing traffic distribution across multiple virtual machines or instances, improving availability and providing redundancy.

Availability sets: ARM enables the creation of availability sets, which distribute virtual machines across fault domains and update domains to ensure high availability and minimize downtime during maintenance or failures.

Virtual machine extensions: ARM supports virtual machine extensions, which can be used to enable auto-scaling, install monitoring agents, configure diagnostics, and perform other tasks to enhance scalability and availability.

Regional redundancy: ARM supports deploying resources to multiple Azure regions, providing geographic redundancy and ensuring high availability in case of regional failures or disasters.

Q450: What is Azure Resource Manager (ARM) template deployment mode, and how does it differ from Azure classic deployment model?

Answer: The Azure Resource Manager (ARM) template deployment mode is the modern approach for deploying and managing Azure resources. Here's how it differs from the classic deployment model:

Resource group-centric: ARM organizes resources into logical groups called resource groups, allowing for easier management, deployment, and monitoring of related resources. The classic model, on the other hand, uses a subscription-centric approach.

Declarative deployment: ARM templates are JSON files that define the desired state of the infrastructure. When deploying using ARM, you declare the desired configuration, and ARM handles the provisioning and management of resources accordingly. The classic model uses imperative scripting for resource provisioning.

Dependency management: ARM automatically handles dependencies between resources, ensuring that resources are provisioned in the correct order. In the classic model, dependencies need to be manually managed.

Role-based access control (RBAC): ARM integrates with Azure Active Directory and provides RBAC, allowing fine-grained access control and management permissions for resources. RBAC was not natively available in the classic model.

Integrated resource tagging and metadata: ARM allows the use of resource tags and metadata, providing a more organized and searchable way to manage and categorize resources. The classic model did not have built-in support for resource tagging.

Q451: What is Azure Blueprints, and how can it help in managing Azure projects?

Answer: Azure Blueprints is a service that helps in creating and managing reusable, composable, and version-controlled templates for deploying Azure environments. Here's how it can help in managing Azure projects:

Standardized deployments: Azure Blueprints allows organizations to define standardized and compliant Azure environments by capturing a set of predefined resources and configurations. This ensures consistent deployments across projects and teams.

Compliance and governance: Azure Blueprints supports policy enforcement, enabling organizations to enforce compliance and governance rules across Azure environments. This helps ensure that deployments meet regulatory and security requirements.

Reusability and consistency: Blueprints provide reusable templates that can be shared across projects and teams, promoting consistency and reducing deployment errors.

Version control and updates: Blueprints can be version-controlled, allowing for easy management and tracking of changes. Updates to blueprints can be rolled out across deployments, ensuring consistency and minimizing manual updates.

Audit and reporting: Azure Blueprints provides visibility into deployed environments, allowing organizations to track and report on the compliance and configuration of Azure resources.

Q452: What is Azure Resource Graph, and how can it assist in querying and analyzing Azure resources?

Answer: Azure Resource Graph is a service that provides fast and efficient querying of Azure resources at scale. Here's how it can assist in querying and analyzing Azure resources:

Fast and efficient queries: Azure Resource Graph allows for complex queries across Azure subscriptions, resource groups, and resource types. It provides faster query response times compared to traditional methods, enabling quick analysis of resource data.

Cross-resource analysis: With Azure Resource Graph, you can query and analyze resources across multiple subscriptions and resource groups, providing a comprehensive view of your Azure environment.

Filter and refine queries: Resource Graph supports filtering and refining queries using various attributes, allowing you to narrow down the results and focus on specific resource types or properties.

Advanced querying capabilities: Resource Graph supports advanced querying capabilities, such as aggregations, sorting, and joining multiple resource types, enabling complex analysis and reporting.

Integration with other Azure services: Azure Resource Graph integrates with other Azure services like Azure Monitor and Azure Policy, allowing you to leverage the query results for monitoring, governance, and compliance purposes.

Q453: What are Azure Resource Manager templates, and how do they simplify deployment and management of Azure resources?

Answer: Azure Resource Manager (ARM) templates are JSON files that define the desired state of Azure resources. Here's how they simplify deployment and management:

Infrastructure as code: ARM templates enable infrastructure provisioning and configuration through code, providing version control, reproducibility, and automation capabilities.

Consistent deployments: Templates ensure consistent deployments by specifying the exact resources, configurations, and dependencies required for the application or infrastructure.

Repeatable deployments: Templates can be reused across environments, projects, and teams, allowing for repeatable deployments that reduce errors and streamline the deployment process.

Parameterization: Templates support parameterization, allowing customization of deployments based on specific requirements without modifying the underlying template.

Automated provisioning: ARM templates can be integrated with deployment tools like Azure DevOps and Azure CLI to automate the provisioning process, reducing manual intervention and saving time.

Q454: What is Azure DevOps, and how can it be used in Azure projects?

Answer: Azure DevOps is a set of development tools and services that facilitate the entire development lifecycle, including planning, coding, testing, and deployment. Here's how it can be used in Azure projects:

Agile planning and tracking: Azure DevOps provides features for backlog management, sprint planning, and task tracking, enabling teams to plan and track their work using agile methodologies.

Version control: Azure DevOps offers version control services like Azure Repos, which support Git repositories, allowing teams to manage and track code changes efficiently.

Continuous Integration and Continuous Deployment (CI/CD): Azure DevOps pipelines enable the implementation of automated CI/CD workflows, including building, testing, and deploying applications to Azure, ensuring faster and more reliable releases.

Testing and quality assurance: Azure DevOps includes testing tools and services like Azure Test Plans, enabling teams to plan, track, and execute test cases and track their results.

Collaboration and communication: Azure DevOps provides features for team collaboration, including dashboards, wikis, and integration with communication tools like Microsoft Teams, facilitating effective communication and knowledge sharing within the project team.

Q455: What are Azure Resource Locks, and how can they be used to protect critical Azure resources?

Answer: Azure Resource Locks are a feature that allows you to lock resources in Azure to prevent accidental deletion or modification. Here's how they can be used:

Read-only lock: A read-only lock allows you to protect a resource from any modification, ensuring that it can only be viewed or read.

Delete lock: A delete lock prevents the accidental deletion of a resource, providing an additional layer of protection against critical resource loss.

Applied at different levels: Resource locks can be applied at the subscription level, resource group level, or individual resource level, allowing for flexible protection based on specific needs.

Governance and compliance: Resource locks help enforce governance and compliance policies by preventing unauthorized changes to critical resources, ensuring adherence to security and compliance requirements.

Collaboration and team coordination: Resource locks can also serve as a coordination mechanism for teams working on shared resources, ensuring that modifications or deletions are done deliberately and with proper coordination.

Q456: What is Azure App Service and how does it simplify the deployment and management of web applications?

Answer: Azure App Service is a fully managed platform for building, deploying, and scaling web applications. Here's how it simplifies deployment and management:

Easy deployment: Azure App Service provides built-in support for deploying various types of web applications, including .NET, Node.js, Java, Python, and more. Deployment can be done directly from source control or through CI/CD pipelines.

Auto-scaling: App Service offers automatic scaling capabilities, allowing applications to handle increased traffic and demands without manual intervention. It can scale horizontally by adding more instances or vertically by adjusting the size of the underlying compute resources.

Built-in security: App Service integrates with Azure Active Directory for authentication and authorization. It also supports SSL certificates, custom domains, and traffic encryption, ensuring the security of web applications.

Continuous deployment: App Service seamlessly integrates with Azure DevOps and other CI/CD tools, enabling continuous deployment workflows. Changes pushed to source control trigger automatic deployments to the App Service environment.

Monitoring and diagnostics: Azure App Service provides built-in monitoring and diagnostics capabilities, allowing you to track the health and performance of your web applications. It integrates with Azure Monitor and Application Insights for deeper insights and analysis.

Q457: What is Azure Logic Apps and how does it facilitate workflow automation and integration?

Answer: Azure Logic Apps is a cloud-based service that allows you to build and automate workflows by integrating various applications, services, and systems. Here's how it facilitates workflow automation and integration:

Connectors: Logic Apps offers a wide range of connectors to connect with popular services like Office 365, Azure services, SaaS applications, and more. These connectors enable seamless integration between different systems.

Visual designer: Logic Apps provides a visual designer that allows you to create workflows using a drag-and-drop interface. It simplifies the process of designing and defining the flow of actions and triggers in the workflow.

Trigger-based execution: Logic Apps can be triggered by various events or actions, such as receiving an email, receiving a message in a queue, or a scheduled time. This trigger-based execution enables workflows to start automatically based on specific conditions.

Conditional branching and transformations: Logic Apps supports conditional branching and transformations, allowing you to define complex logic within your workflows. You can perform data transformations, apply conditional statements, and handle exceptions within the workflow.

Monitoring and tracking: Logic Apps provides monitoring and tracking capabilities, allowing you to monitor the execution status, track the progress of workflows, and troubleshoot any issues that may arise during the execution.

Q458: What is Azure API Management and how does it help in managing and securing APIs?

Answer: Azure API Management is a service that enables organizations to create, publish, secure, and manage APIs at scale. Here's how it helps in managing and securing APIs:

API gateway: API Management acts as an API gateway, providing a single entry point for accessing multiple APIs. It handles authentication, authorization, traffic management, and caching, simplifying API consumption.

API lifecycle management: API Management offers tools to manage the full lifecycle of APIs, including versioning, documentation, testing, and deployment. It provides a centralized platform for managing APIs across different stages of development.

Security and access control: API Management allows you to secure your APIs by providing authentication and authorization mechanisms. It supports various authentication protocols, such as OAuth 2.0 and JWT, and enables fine-grained access control through policies.

Rate limiting and throttling: API Management helps in managing API usage by enforcing rate limits and throttling policies. This ensures fair usage of APIs and prevents abuse or overload.

Analytics and monitoring: API Management provides analytics and monitoring capabilities, allowing you to gain insights into API usage, performance, and errors. It helps in identifying trends, optimizing API design, and troubleshooting issues.

KS EBOOKS

About the Ebook

Interview Mastery: 460 Questions & Answers" is the ultimate guide

AZURE INTERVIEW QUESTIONS

to help you crack any interview and land your dream job. Packed with practical tips and strategies, this book is designed for both students and experienced professionals looking to enhance their interview skills. It features real-time interview questions and provides hands-on advice for troubleshooting common issues. Gain confidence, stand out from the competition, and secure your desired position with this indispensable resource.

www.ksebooks.com

Printed in Great Britain
by Amazon